Fire Walk With Me:
Your Laura Disappeared

ALSO BY SCOTT RYAN

SCOTT LUCK STORIES
(2014)

THIRTYSOMETHING AT THIRTY: AN ORAL HISTORY
(2017)

THE LAST DAYS OF LETTERMAN
(2019)

BUT, COULDN'T I DO THAT? ANSWERING YOUR QUESTIONS ABOUT SELF-PUBLISHING (WITH ERIN O'NEIL)
(2021)

MOONLIGHTING: AN ORAL HISTORY
(2021)

LOST HIGHWAY: THE FIST OF LOVE
(2023)

THE LAST DECADE OF CINEMA
(2024)

ALWAYS MUSIC IN THE AIR: THE SOUNDS OF TWIN PEAKS
(2025)

EDITED BY SCOTT RYAN

THE BLUE ROSE MAGAZINE
(2017-CURRENT)

THE WOMEN OF DAVID LYNCH
(2019)

THE WOMEN OF AMY SHERMAN-PALLADINO
(2020)

TWIN PEAKS UNWRAPPED
(WRITTEN BY BEN DURANT & BRYON KOZACZKA)
(2020)

MASSILLON TIGERS: 15 FOR 15
(WRITTEN BY DAVID LEE MORGAN, JR.)
(2020)

MYTH OR MAYOR: THE SEARCH FOR MY FAMILY'S LEGACY
(WRITTEN BY ALEX RYAN/AFTERWORD BY SCOTT RYAN)
(2021)

Fire Walk With Me:
Your Laura Disappeared

Scott Ryan

FAYETTEVILLE
MAFIA
PRESS

Cover design by Scott Ryan
Cover photos courtesy of New Line Cinema, Scott Ryan
All photos/screen captures from *FWWM* are courtesy of New Line Cinema.
All photos/screen captures from *Twin Peaks* are courtesy of CBS.
Original art by Maja Ljunggren
Author photo by Faye Murman

Edited by David Bushman
Book designed by Scott Ryan

Published in the USA by Fayetteville Mafia Press
Columbus, Ohio

Contact Information
Email: fayettevillemafiapress@gmail.com
Website: TuckerDSPresss.com
Twitter: @FMPBooks
Instagram: @Fayettevillemafiapress

ISBN: 9781949024241
eBook ISBN: 9781949024258

“He smiles sweetly
Strokes my hair, says he misses me.
I would murder him right there
But first I die.”

—Stephen Sondheim
“Every Day a Little Death,” *A Little Night Music*

“Bob is real.”

— Laura Palmer
Fire Walk With Me

CONTENTS

ABBREVIATIONS IN THE BOOK

FWWM - *Fire Walk With Me*
MFAP - Man From Another Place/Mike
TRATCS - The Room Above the Convenience Store
OAM - One-Armed Man
TOS - The Original Series (which means *Twin Peaks* Seasons 1 & 2)
BRM - *The Blue Rose* magazine (2017-)
CWMF - *Conversations With Mark Frost (2020)*
RRP - *The Red Room Podcast*
VTTP - *Voyage to Twin Peaks* documentary (2017)
FBL - Facebook Live - *Blue Rose* Facebook page (2020)
TPU book - *Twin Peaks Unwrapped* book (2020)
Script1 - *FWWM* script from July 3, 1991 (no Chet Desmond)
Script2 - *FWWM* script from August 8, 1991 (Chet & Cooper)

This book is dedicated to the angels who saved me:

Jen,

Lisa,

Courtenay,

Janet,

Sheryl Lee,

and

Catherine Coulson.

FOREWORD
BY JEFF JENSEN

Twin Peaks: Fire Walk With Me, David Lynch's sixth motion picture, released in 1992, was a cinematic expansion of the supernatural soap opera that the director began with Mark Frost two years earlier on TV and a furiously combustible paradox, a decidedly difficult labor of love that burned for our life-giving attention even as it wantonly defied our desires of it. It remains a vibrant yet volatile work of art that fumes with resentment over its very existence, maybe now more than ever, albeit for different reasons: where once it was a movie of its time that mourned the untimely passing of the initial incarnation of *Twin Peaks*, it's now a thing unstuck in time, its meanings in flux due to the dizzying retcons produced by the 2017 franchise revival. "I am dead . . . and yet I live," seethed Laura Palmer early in *Twin Peaks: The Return*. She was speaking of her spectral residency in the limbo realm of The Black Lodge. But in her anger, I hear a complaint about the price she and the movie that gave her better immortality than simply being a corpse wrapped in plastic were going to have to pay to give the men in her life—yes, Agent Dale Cooper, but Lynch-Frost, too—the chance to play hero in the culture again. Regardless, I can't think of a better line to sum up the captivating and confounding thing *Fire Walk With Me* has always been, and should always be.

An unconventional prequel film before prequel films were conventional, *FWWM* wasn't something most people wanted back in the day. Not the critics who wanted Lynch to put the small screen behind him and get back to painting fresh, original, big-screen *Blue Velvets*. Not the fans who stuck with *Twin Peaks* through two turbulent seasons and were left hanging with unsolved mysteries and unresolved storylines. Not Frost, who thought it was a dubious and unnecessary idea and declined to participate; and really not even Agent Cooper himself, Kyle MacLachlan, who participated reluctantly, and even then, for a handful of shooting days, a complication that, as Scott Ryan expertly investigates in the pages to come, altered Lynch's vision of the movie and contributed to its fractured, chaotic personality.

To borrow an idea from *The Return*'s additions to *Twin Peaks* mythology, *FWWM* has always been, for me, Tulpa *Twin Peaks*—a doppelgänger that resembles *Twin Peaks* in form and spirit, and yet is not *Twin Peaks*, not really. It's a golem *Twin Peaks* made to serve other masters and interests than the original thing from which it was made; an uncanny valley *Twin Peaks*, buggy and haunted by what it's not and what's missing, even as it tries to replace those things with surrogates and recastings: Chris Isaak's Chet Desmond doing Dale Cooper's sleuthing work, Moira Kelly filling the knee-highs of Lara Flynn Boyle.

The making-of lore asserts that Lynch chose Laura Palmer as *FWWM's* subject—despite (and maybe in spite of?) the target market's pressing interests ("*How's Annie? HOW'S ANNIE?!*")—because he ardently loved the character and believed there was enough unsaid about the existential crisis of her horror-show life to support a supple work of cinema and single-serving expression of *Twin Peaks*.

This ambition is certainly more acceptable in light of at least one favor that *The Return* does for the prequel: No longer the frustrating final word on *Twin Peaks*, *FWWM* can now fully be what Lynch maybe always wanted, a freaky, unique thing that exists unto itself and for itself, a portrait of a young woman under psychic, physical, sexual, and spiritual siege, desperate to escape into a reality where she can live free. And those of us who've long struggled with *FWWM*—and yes, that *was* a confession—must acknowledge that Lynch's mission was thoroughly realized from the jump thanks to the spectacular achievement his cameras captured: Sheryl Lee's gutsy, deeply felt, incendiary performance, a bravura turn that was underrecognized upon release, but has gained in renown and luster in the decades since.

That said, I don't *feel* Lynch's passion for Laura Palmer in *FWWM.*

What I *do* feel—preserved on celluloid for all time—is *garmonbozia*—pain and sorrow—over the cancellation of *Twin Peaks*, which I submit is the film's true subject. You feel this funk and fury from the get-go, with opening credits that roll over bluesy static set to a sad saxophone wail that ends with a jolt of violence: Lynch pulls back to reveal we've been watching a TV set, which is then attacked and destroyed by an unseen assailant, who then turns his violent attentions to an unseen woman. Her scream sends us into the story proper, such as it is.

Like Lynch's twenty-first-century masterpiece *Mulholland Dr.*—a transcendent salvage of a failed TV pilot—*FWWM* is a requiem for a dream that was always folly, the want to tell a never-ending story. Of *course* the prequel had to be about Laura Palmer: she was the perfect metaphor for the brief, beautiful, betrayed, blown up life of *Twin Peaks* itself. By resurrecting her to delight in her one more time—and giving her agency, heroic achievement, and ascension into an afterlife attended by literal angels—Lynch produced an ecstatic, cathartic, redemptive ritual of mourning that remains potent to this day, even as its identity and legacy have been complicated by *The Return*. The film's ragged edges—its absences and fragmentations, its dementedness and dissatisfactions, and now even its status as an unmoored, unsettled thing—actually serve its best meaning, which is also the meaning of the entire franchise: *Twin Peaks*, in all its forms, was, is, and will always be one of the great pieces of pop art about the screaming, shattering experience of grief and all of its world-destroying—and world-creating—power.

In the same way *FWWM* honored *Twin Peaks*, *Fire Walk With Me: Your Laura Disappeared* honors *FWWM* here on the occasion of its thirtieth anniversary. Scott's book is also a tribute to his tribe, the contingent of fans that kept *Twin Peaks* from vanishing from the culture in the decades prior to *The Return* with thoughtful, loving theorizing—published first in fanzines, then on the web—while also respecting the fundamental mystery of *Twin Peaks* and having a pretty good sense of humor about themselves too. An accomplished entertainment journalist with an eclectic array of interests (his recent oral history of *Moonlighting* is another must read), Scott brings his A game to an endeavor that's as personal as it is professional: his testimony of *Twin Peaks* fandom is the origin story of a great many contemporary scholars of pop culture (present company included) who had their imaginations captured not just with *Twin Peaks*, but with the creative potential for TV as well as cinema. He has given us a book to nurture our endless explorations of *Twin Peaks* and occupy our time during this new stretch of "Meanwhile . . . " waiting, the default orientation of *Twin Peaks* appreciation, the frozen pose of our inextinguishable fire, our blazing queen, our Laura. Long may she yet live.

See you again in 25 years?

> Jeff Jensen is the former TV critic of *Entertainment Weekly* and cohost of *A Twin Peaks Podcast: A Podcast About Twin Peaks*. He's also a writer of TV shows (HBO's *Watchmen*) and graphic novels. His new book, *Better Angels: A Kate Warne Adventure*, is in stores now.

Original Art by Maja Ljunggren.

INTRODUCTION

You Made Me Write It All Down

If you opened this book hoping to read about how David Lynch's 1992 feature film *Twin Peaks: Fire Walk With Me* (*FWWM*) was booed at the Cannes Film Fest, you've got the wrong book. If you want a straight retelling of the film, just pop it in your Blu-ray player and watch it. If you want a rehash of Quentin Tarantino's misguided critique or Roger Ebert's negative review of the film, *yaw gnorw* (wrong way) again. All the above, despite the fact that *FWWM* was, upon its release, the least commercially successful part of the *Twin Peaks* canon, has been covered time and time again. The original run of the *Twin Peaks* television series (TOS) rocked pop culture in 1990, *Twin Peaks: The Return* gave Showtime its biggest new-customer sign-up day in company history in 2017, but *FWWM* opened and closed at the box office faster than a pine weasel scampers through Glastonbury Grove. I am proud to present a thirtieth-anniversary celebration of the film because, just like Laura Palmer, it didn't go away quietly. There is no better way to celebrate *FWWM* than with something new that has a little bit of everything—interviews, essays, comedy, nonsense, sadness, and deep thoughts—you know, just like the film. The reason a movie that grossed under $10 million at the box office is still alive and well today is because of . . . well, fans like me.

I saw *FWWM* in the theater on opening night, August 28, 1992, at a single-screen movie house called Park Cinema. The reason I know that is because I took a picture of the outdoor marquee. Do you have any idea how rare it was to take a camera somewhere in 1992? We just didn't do that. People looked at me strangely because I had a camera in the parking lot of a movie theater. It's an example of how much life has changed since the film was released. In today's world, we are instructed to shut our cameras (phones) off before a film starts because everyone brings one. But to me, it was so insane that *Twin Peaks* actually came to my small town of Massillon, Ohio, that I needed to capture it on Kodak. I saw the movie Friday and again on Wednesday the following week, and by the next Friday, the film was gone, like a turkey in the corn. It

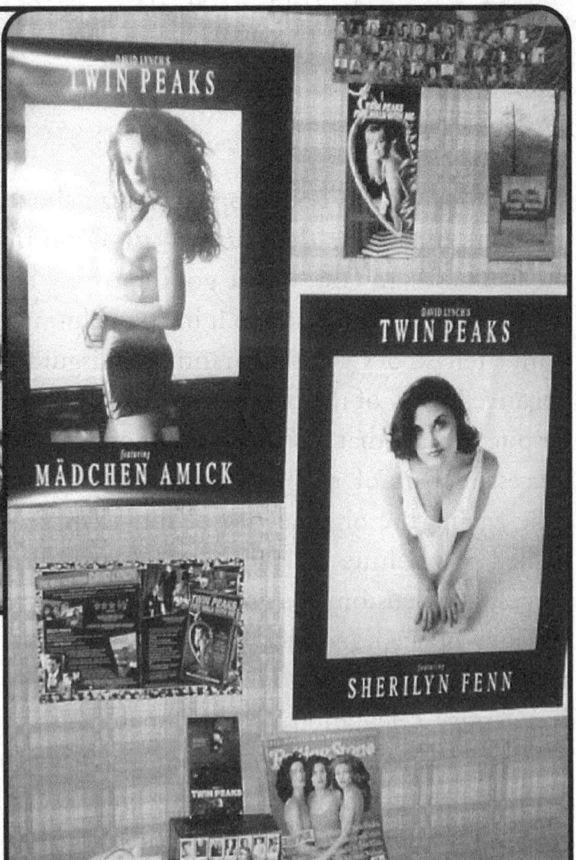

The *FWWM* marquee in 1992 and my *Twin Peaks* wall in 1993 (yes, those are CD longboxes for you Gen X-ers). Photos by Scott Ryan

coincidentally stayed for only seven days, which matched the tagline on the script—"the last seven days of Laura Palmer."

Everyone I saw the film with on that opening night hated it. Everyone I knew was disappointed in it. Every review I read of the film slammed it. If you ever get a chance to read any interviews Lynch gave in 1992 or the transcript of the Cannes press conference, you will feel the complete hatred the press had for the film. It wasn't just that they didn't like the film; it was also that David Lynch truly angered them. The questions were hostile. They were annoyed with his answers (or lack of them), and you could tell they truly just didn't get the film. FYI, there wasn't one question about sexual abuse. Critics missed the point of the movie by a mile.

When I went to see it for the second time at that Wednesday afternoon matinee, I was the only person in the theater. That has never happened to me again in my life. (Creepy side note: the manager of the cinema walked into the theater when Bob crawled through the window and watched just that entire scene. That made it even more disturbing to me.) I didn't even tell my girlfriend I was going to see it again, because she hated the film so much. I didn't want to admit how much I loved it. I wondered if there was something wrong with me that I was, seemingly, the only person who loved it. Well, "loved" isn't quite right. How could anyone *love* it on first viewing? It's such an emotional beating. A more apt description might be that I couldn't look away from it. There was something there that was so remarkably different from the series or anything else I had watched. If you ask *Twin Peaks* fans in 2022 how they feel about *FWWM*, almost all of them will say it's a masterpiece. (Don't ask *Reflections: An Oral History of Twin Peaks* author Brad Dukes, but besides him, almost everyone will say they loved it the first time they saw it. They lie.)

The movie has been reassessed over time even though not a frame of it has changed. It isn't that the movie changed; it's just that the audience finally caught up to the story and the difficult art that David Lynch served us. In May 2021, I was fortunate enough to host a Q and A with some of the cast of *Twin Peaks* before a drive-in screening of *FWWM*. Over a thousand people attended the sold-out Mahoning Drive-in event. People dressed up as Agent Cooper, Laura in The Red Room, Nadine Hurley as a cheerleader, tons of Log Ladies, and Double R waitresses. As

The Mahoning Drive-in screens *FWWM*. Photo courtesy of Faye Murman

I walked among the crowd, I thought it was insane all these people were there for a movie that lost at the box office to *Honeymoon in Vegas*. People were so happy to be there—to get to see in 35mm on a big screen a film about the murder and sexual abuse of a daughter at the hands of her father. For this, people were dressing up, having doughnuts, and braving the COVID world? It was so evident, in that dusty parking lot in the conservative state of Pennsylvania, how this film had overcome the initial reaction thirty years before and only gotten better with age, received more respect, and done the unthinkable—made viewers confront the horror of incest. This wasn't at an art house theater in New York or LA. No, this was in Middle America, where people were scarfing down nachos and hot dogs, not caviar. They announced it was the drive-in's largest ever crowd. Did I mention that when I saw the film for the second time, I was the only person in the theater? What happened over the thirty years between these showings?

FWWM became less confusing to viewers. Its story became clearer with repeat viewings, and with the help of a plethora of essays by *Twin Peaks* scholars decoding the film. I have no plans to explain the movie to any reader. That would be against my *Twin Peaks* rules. Figuring Lynch out is what you do alone. I want to take a look at where the movie stands in 2022 and how it was created in 1992. To view it as a piece of living art, which I believe film is. Film reflects society in the moment that the film is watched, not just when it is made. That's why movies shift in and out of vogue. *FWWM* took the subject of incest and brought it to the big screen. In 1992, we were ending twelve solid years of the Reagan/Republican era. America wasn't ready for the story director David Lynch and actress Sheryl Lee were telling. Today's audiences can handle darker material. In fact, they demand it.

I will not be partaking in what I call Lynchsplaining: the act of a fan explaining to another what Lynch meant when he constructed a scene. I don't believe that can be done. Anyone who tries to Lynchsplain always comes out on the wrong end of the sycamore stick. Only Lynch knows why the monkey says Judy at the end of the film. If you want to know why, figure it out. Or if you are really brave, ask Lynch. But I am pretty damn sure he isn't gonna tell you. Let me give you an example of why Lynchsplaining can be a deceptive act to partake in. Here is a word salad I freestyled just to prove how you can explain anything in a Lynch film. If you ask me, "Yo, Scott, why does the monkey say Judy?" I can easily say this:

> *The monkey wears the same mask that the little boy, Pierre Tremond, wears. This little boy represents Leland Palmer as a child, who succumbs to his animal instincts; therefore he is represented by a monkey. Everyone knows that a child will always rebel against what they are told. That is a classic act of youth. A youth who invited Bob inside him would have those feelings even more. So when Phillip Jeffries says "We're not gonna talk about Judy" to Agent Cooper and Gordon Cole, Leland as a petulant youth, represented by the monkey, has to respond with "Judy." This correlates with breaking the ultimate rule, which is to not abuse your child. This is actually him admitting that he raped his own daughter.*

See? Nonsense. I just made that up off the top of my head. I have never considered any of that before and spent no time on it. But I tied together many open plot points of the film or the mythology and connected them to things that happened in the series or film. You can make any part of a Lynch film seem like it is saying *something*. You just have to tie it to another open plot point. Lynch purposely leaves space in his art for you to connect your own thoughts. But that doesn't mean you *have* to. I will be pointing out connections that are in the film and the series, but will not be pushing theories that can't be proved. (Feel free to steal my "Monkey Says Judy" theory and develop it. There might be something there.)

Instead of Lynchsplaining, I interview several of the principal players who created *FWWM* and discuss my personal journey with the movie. *FWWM* was a movie that I strangely watched every year on my birthday from 1993 to 1997. I have never been sexually assaulted, and I don't identify with that aspect of the torture and cruelty Laura Palmer experienced, but I did strongly identify with her sadness and duality. Over time, that journey has deepened for me. It always feels strange to pick *FWWM* as my all-time favorite movie, because it is an excruciatingly hard piece of art to digest. Yet it is the movie I have seen the most times. (Unless you count *The Little Mermaid*, which played nonstop when I worked at a video store in the early nineties.) I can speak only to what this film means to me, what I have learned in studying it for thirty years, in covering *Twin Peaks* as a podcaster for thirteen years, as a writer on the subject for over a decade, and as the managing editor of *The Blue Rose* for five years.

The first thing I officially published about *Twin Peaks* was in *Twin Peaks Fan Phenomena* (2013). My brother-in-law Josh Minton and I coauthored an essay called "Yeah, But The Monkey Says Judy." (Looks like that theory has been brewing in my subconscious for years.) In it we said something that I still believe wholeheartedly. The only reliable narrator in *FWWM* is the sound. To prove to you how recent the new way of looking at *FWWM* is, the only reason we were chosen to be in *Twin Peaks Fan Phenomena* was because despite the multitude of entries for the book, we were the only people who pitched an essay about the film. And this was back when the only true canon options were the original series (TOS) and *FWWM*. None of the other writers wanted to write about *FWWM*. I am proud that we wrote our essay before the world reassessed the film. It is true most of the things we pointed out have now been covered to death in today's world of podcasts galore, but they were new ideas at the time. I think my grandma just started a podcast on *Twin Peaks*. It's pretty good. She built an entire episode around my monkey-says-Judy theory and snagged a three-hour interview with Harry Goaz.

So, enough about what is not in this book. What is in it? The first two chapters set the stage for the film and how it shaped me. In Chapter 3, I bring in some of the actors and crew from the different interviews I have conducted or my various companies have published over the years. Chapter 4 has my first-ever interview with Gregg Fienberg, who produced the film and worked on the original series. Chapter 5 is a comparison between the shooting script and the original draft of the film. This is the most nerdy, in-depth chapter in the book and is for hard-core fans only. It really gets into the trees, and I learned so much studying how the film evolved from concept to finished product. One of the things that I have learned in studying this film is that Lynch was still figuring out what he wanted to say and do all the way up to the editing process. Going back to the sound, I pick a few tracks from the score by Angelo Badalamenti in Chapter 6 and analyze the music from the film. Chapter 7 has a brand-new interview with Ron Garcia, who was the cinematographer of the film. I then cover the deleted scenes, followed by a look at how the cutting of one of those scenes confused European viewers for decades. In Chapter 10, I talk with the editor of the film, Mary Sweeney, and then I write about my journey with the film and my lifelong desire to interview Sheryl Lee. The final chapter is a brand-new interview with Sheryl Lee.

Over the past thirty years, the one thing that remained the golden orb of the film to me is Sheryl Lee's performance as Laura Palmer. I remember how it affected me the very first time and has every time since. It was what made me lie to my girlfriend and sneak back to the theater to see the film again that first week. It is hard to measure the quality of art. Who can say that Dustin Hoffman in *Rain Man* is better than Robert De Niro in *Goodfellas*? Or that Meryl Streep in *Postcards from the Edge* is better than Uma Thurman in *Kill Bill*? No one can. Although I *can* and often do say that Sheryl Lee gives the best performance ever captured on film in *FWWM*. There really isn't anything else like it. One of the main reasons this movie haunted me for twenty-five of the last thirty years is because I couldn't comprehend how Sheryl Lee did what she did, or gave what she gave. I wanted to know so badly how anyone could emote such honesty on film. Over the past five years, I have inexplicably been fortunate enough to get to know Sheryl Lee. That is one question in a world of blue that has been answered. I no longer am baffled by what Sheryl Lee did. I know how she did it. She did it because she is just that *good*. She is that honest. She is **and isn't** Laura Palmer. It is as confounding as "She's dead, yet she lives." That. Is. Sheryl. Lee.

Meeting her on February 24, 2018, to conduct an interview for *The Blue Rose* #8, and then forging a friendship with her, has been a dream come true. It not only helped me to understand how she was able to achieve such an acting feat, but also brought a truly inspiring human into my life. I had put the character of Laura Palmer on such a high pedestal for so many years. When I finally met the person behind the mask, I realized that I had gained and lost something. I gained a friend and lost an icon. I am more than OK with that. In fact, when I realized how it was Sheryl's honesty and ability to share emotion with others that brought Laura Palmer to life, I thought to myself, "Your Laura disappeared."

CHAPTER 1

When This Kind of Fire Starts

As someone who watched *Twin Peaks* when it originally aired, I will never forget the pit in my stomach when Agent Cooper smashes the mirror and sees Bob as his reflection. The hero became the villain and the series ended. It would be impossible to explain to someone today how much *Twin Peaks* had fallen out of favor in 1991. *Twin Peaks,* like Laura Palmer, had died, but unlike with the homecoming queen, no one cared about the death. Viewers had moved on. I couldn't. I thought about it nonstop. There was no hope. I never expected to see new *Twin Peaks* again. Heck, I never expected to get to see the series again. There was no such thing as a TV show released on home video at that time. All I had was the second season, which I had taped directly off ABC, and most of that had news flashes about the first Gulf War all over the screen.

The final episode of the series aired on June 10, 1991, and it was full of cliffhangers. Audrey Horne explodes in a bank, Doc Hayward smashes Ben Horne into the fireplace mantel, Cooper is Bob, and poor Leo Johnson is left clinching a rope with his teeth as tight as he can so spiders won't fall on his face. (Well, maybe not all the plots were top-notch.) But there was another cliffhanger, which none of us focused on that night. With eighteen minutes left in the final episode, there is a scene between Agent Cooper and Laura Palmer in The Red Room. Laura says, "I'll see you again in twenty-five years. Meanwhile." And then she freezes in a pose. This is, comically, the cliffhanger David Lynch and Mark Frost, cocreators of the series, picked up when *Twin Peaks* returned to television in 2017. All the soap opera cliffhangers were never explained. As a twenty-one-year-old college student, I wasn't focusing on Laura saying "I'll see you in twenty-five years." I was focusing on why my Audrey was blown to bits. I needed to know that she was alive and well. But Lynch famously told *Eyes on Cinema* in 2015, and then repeated it in promotions for *The Return* in 2017, "Keep your eye on the doughnut, not on the hole." Well, in 1991, I was doughnut bound.

This was the genesis of the problem filmgoers had with *FWWM* in 1992. They weren't looking at what they were given (the doughnut). They were focused on what was missing (the hole). The hole, in this case, was solving the mysteries of Cooper as Bob, Audrey's explosion, and (albeit for only a few, strange people who were still wondering about it) Leo and

Laura Palmer strikes a pose. Photo courtesy of CBS Home Video

his dangling spider cage. Focusing on the hole caused disappointment. While the rest of fandom focused on the plot points in 1992, David Lynch was concentrating on something else. He was baking up a tasty doughnut to give us the backstory of Laura Palmer and what she went through to bring us entry to the town of Twin Peaks. The reason I didn't focus on Laura's quote was because I knew why she had said she would see Agent Cooper in twenty-five years. Lynch wasn't thinking that he and Mark Frost would go back to the series a quarter of a century later. He was referencing the dream that aired in Episode 2 of Season 1 in which Cooper met Laura Palmer in The Red Room and appeared older. That same dream sequence was used as a closed ending for the European home video release of the pilot episode of *Twin Peaks*. During that scene, there was a subtitle that never aired in America. It says at the bottom of the screen: TWENTY-FIVE YEARS LATER.

So twenty-five years later was not an example of Lynch seeing into the future; Lynch was referencing something he had directed in the past. So that is still not one of the cliffhangers for David Lynch. I like thinking

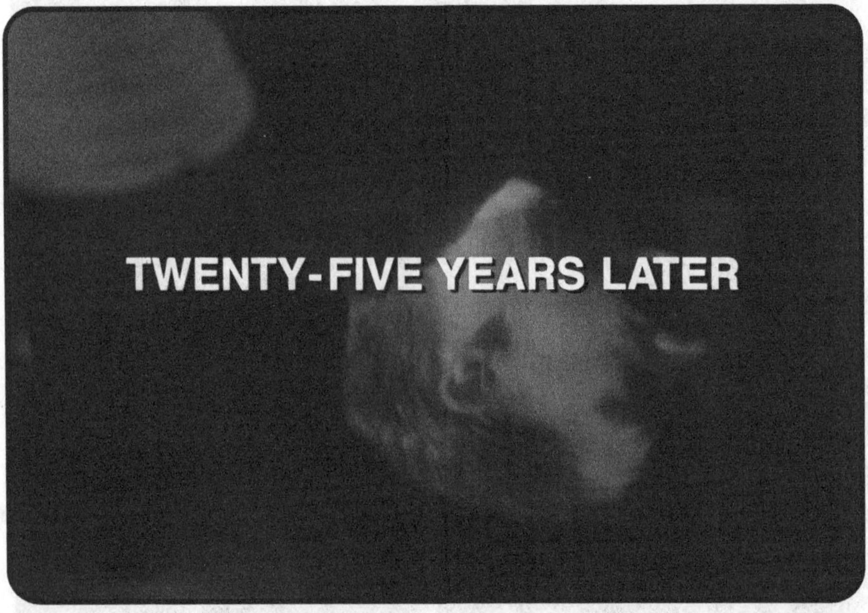

A screen capture from the European ending of the pilot, which was not originally released in America. Photo courtesy of CBS Home Video

that it was Laura's next word, which I admit I didn't focus on in 1991, "meanwhile," that really sparked Lynch to want to study more about Laura Palmer. A simple word to be ignored when stacked up against all the other crazy that was going on in that episode. But it is the idea that excites Lynch. He said in his book *Catching the Big Fish*, "Ideas are like fish. If you want to catch little fish, you can stay in the shallow water. But if you want to catch the big fish, you've got to go deeper. Down deep, the fish are more powerful and more pure. They're huge and abstract. And they're very beautiful." To me, *FWWM* is the "meanwhile." Lynch wanted you to focus on Laura Palmer for a while and forget about Cooper/Bob and the rest of the story. Laura is the one. *FWWM* is the doughnut. The viewer's wish for answers to the cliffhangers is the hole.

David Lynch is obsessed with Laura Palmer. (I guess that puts me in good company.) To him, Laura Palmer is the center of *Twin Peaks*. Mark Frost said in David Bushman's 2019 book *Conversations with Mark Frost*, "Part of this was that Lynch couldn't let go of Laura Palmer as a character. There was something about her that just possessed him. That became a little bit more his obsession than mine." Each episode of *The Return* begins with her face. The end credits of the final episode of the original run has her face in a cup of coffee. The star of *FWWM*? To quote Harriet Hayward, "It was Laura." Lynch was the one who brought her back in the final episode. This was Sheryl Lee's first appearance in the series since her character of Laura's twin cousin, Maddy Ferguson, had died. When Lynch, who famously freestyled the final episode as he filmed it, was given the final hour of the series to direct, he brought back Laura. When he was given the chance to direct a movie, he brought her back. He snapped his fingers backward and said, "Meanwhile, let me present you with the final seven days of Laura Palmer's life."

What seems so wrong for me as a fan who lived through this era is the fact that the time between the final episode and the shooting script of *FWWM* is only two damn months. I don't know how that is even possible. I guess the next time I yell at my kids for being such impatient millennials I will have to remind myself that the finished shooting script of *FWWM* is dated August 8, 1991, which is a whole fifty-nine days from when the Season 2 finale aired on ABC. Part of the reason that it seemed so long between the two is there was such an absence of hope.

Let's not forget that television wasn't rebooting itself back on the big *or* small screen in 1991. Franchises were restricted to Arby's or McDonald's, not failed ABC series. I remember my despair the night of June 10. I was hopeless. Also, when filming started in fall of 1991, I certainly didn't know about it. There was no internet to tell someone in Ohio what was going on in Washington State. I didn't find out about *FWWM* until there was a *TV Guide* article about it in early 1992. So it was longer for me; therefore I will resume yelling at my kids for being millennials.

The other thing that happened during that time frame was that the world was not in David Lynch's corner. He went from being on the cover of *Time* magazine and winning the Palme d'Or for *Wild at Heart* in 1990 to being canceled on ABC in 1991—twice. Once for *Twin Peaks* and once for *On the Air*, another series from Frost and Lynch, which was canceled the moment it aired. (ABC hated it so badly it might have been canceled *before* it aired.) Things change fast at the top, and Lynch just wasn't the media's darling in 1991-92. And it wasn't just critics and viewers; some cast members felt that way about him too. In 2015 when *Twin Peaks* was revived, the cast begged to come back. But in 1991, there was a triad of actors who wanted nothing to do with *Twin Peaks*. Kyle MacLachlan (Agent Cooper), Sherilyn Fenn (Audrey Horne), and Lara Flynn Boyle (Donna Hayward) all famously passed when offered the chance to reprise their characters for David Lynch in *FWWM*.

The fact that Fenn, Boyle, and MacLachlan didn't want to participate is an interesting coincidence that needs to be mentioned, because as Cooper said in Episode 4, "Gentlemen, when two separate events occur simultaneously pertaining to the same object of inquiry, we must always pay strict attention." During the run of *Twin Peaks*, MacLachlan and Boyle dated. It was that relationship that caused the storyline between Cooper and Audrey to be derailed, because Boyle didn't want her boyfriend to make out with Fenn. Sherilyn Fenn has confirmed this rumor multiple times, including in her interview with me on *The Red Room Podcast* #114. She said, "I think it was a dumb reason to pull the characters apart, based on very petty, unprofessional things. There was nothing unprofessional about this sweet organic relationship that developed between two characters on the set. I think the reason for stopping [the Audrey/Cooper relationship] was dumb."

Sherilyn Fenn ended the series chained to a bank vault and passed on returning for *FWWM*. Photo courtesy of CBS Home Video

So even some members of the cast were not interested in going back. Many of the younger actors had become huge stars, and they, rightly so, wanted to go off and do something new and big. Films that were released with those younger actors in 1992-93 included *Wayne's World*, *Six Degrees of Separation*, *Stephen King's Sleepwalkers*, *A Few Good Men*, and *Of Mice and Men*. Kyle MacLachlan had starred in Oliver Stone's *The Doors*, which came out in 1991 as *Twin Peaks* was whimpering to its first end. Robert Engels, cowriter of the *FWWM* script, said that Lynch was surprised when MacLachlan turned the role down. Engels told me, "Kyle didn't want to do it because he didn't want to be Agent Cooper all his life. My point to Kyle was to quote Sean Connery's advice to Christopher Reeve. Reeve didn't want to do another *Superman* movie. Sean said, 'I decided to do James Bond until they didn't want me to do James Bond, and then I would find out if I could act. I was gonna milk that cow till they closed the dairy.' [Laughs.] I am not an actor, but I get that fear of being typecast. Kyle is a fantastic actor and he has done so many funny, strange, and good things. I think he just wanted to play other parts."

This was confirmed on July 12, 1991, in an article by Matt Roush for *USA Today*. Roush wrote, "The long-discussed feature-film companion to ABC's defunct cult series has fallen apart. A major stumbling block: Kyle MacLachlan's reluctance to continue as FBI special agent Dale Cooper." Lynch production spokesman Ken Scherer was quoted as saying, "David really wanted to do it with Kyle, but unfortunately . . . he would like to move away from the character and *Twin Peaks*. We can't do it without him."

MacLachlan came around eventually and performed a limited role in the film. Lara Flynn Boyle passed, and the Donna character was played by Moira Kelly (*The Cutting Edge*, *Chaplin*). Audrey Horne did not appear in the film. One person who didn't mind reprising her role was Sheryl Lee. She was interested in fleshing out the character and working with Lynch again. Lee also has trouble placing linear time to the space between the series finale, which was filmed in March 1991, and the start of the filming of *FWWM* in Snoqualmie, Washington, in September 1991. In the bonus footage for the Criterion release of the film, she says, "I don't ever remember one time specifically where David called me and said, 'Now this is happening.' For me, it was more a memory of a long creative, explorative process. I have no sense of time from when that started until when we started filming . . . because Laura's life is all connected. . . . For me, it is all one memory, because it's all one life."

The last time viewers had seen Laura Palmer, she was frozen in a "meanwhile" pose. Now she would come to life for seven days, only to die again. This time, we would have a front-row seat to her destruction. This was the idea that Lynch caught from the deeper side of the idea lake. He tossed back continuing the story of *Twin Peaks*, and instead plunged in deeper. The doughnut started to take shape. But what about that "meanwhile"?

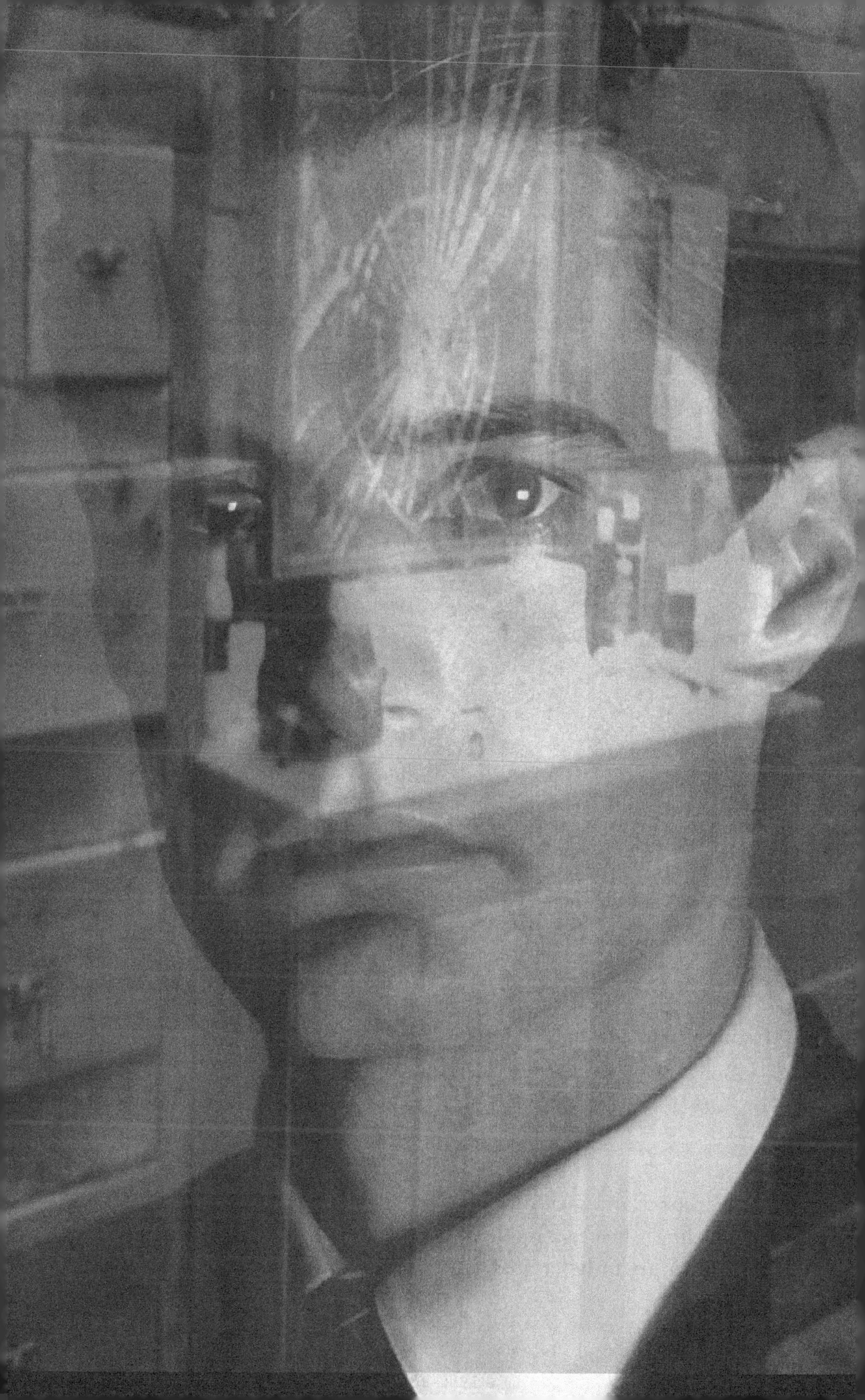

CHAPTER 2

I.

"In the meanwhile,
There are mouths to be kissed
Before mouths to be fed."
—Stephen Sondheim
"The Miller's Son," *A Little Night Music*

"I want to taste through your mouth."
—Bob
Fire Walk With Me

Art inspires art. Each time an artist sets their ideas on paper, canvas, or film, it makes a ripple in the art world. *Twin Peaks* inspired so much other art to be created. That is true in the fan community, but also in Hollywood. I have interviewed Damon Lindelof (*Lost*) and Jeff Lemire (*Sweet Tooth*) about how *Twin Peaks* inspired their television series. Because I always have *Twin Peaks* on my brain, I see connections to song lyrics all the time that make me think of the series. My main inspiration comes from the words of Broadway composer Stephen Sondheim. For every book, I pick a lyric that swims in my mind while I work on the project. For this one, it was two songs from the 1973 musical *A Little Night Music*, "The Miller's Son" and "Every Day a Little Death." One song because I picked it, and one because the siren of *Twin Peaks* brought it to my attention. Now both songs remind me of Laura Palmer.

"The Miller's Son" has the recurring phrase "In the meanwhile." In the context of that song, it's what happens between this point of your life and the next. We live in the meanwhile. ("We live inside a dream.") The character who sings the song is Petra, who wants to have experienced all that life has to offer before she settles down. The song is written for a young woman who refuses to just wait around for a husband. She plans to live life as it happens and take chances. She belts out, "But I'll not have been dead when I die!" Laura Palmer says in *The Return*, "I am dead, yet I live." Laura would have loved this song. *Twin Peaks* alum Julee Cruise not only loves this song, but also sang it on Broadway when she played the part of Petra in a 1985 revival of *A Little Night Music*.

Julee Cruise told me over email, "I love Stephen Sondheim. I am a belter and a Broadway baby. I stopped the show singing 'The Miller's Son.' 'In the meanwhile' was, for me, the dreams for the character. The song and the character of Petra just scream youth. We are wild at heart in our youth, no matter what age." I was so excited that Cruise wanted to talk about the meaning of "The Miller's Son" with me. In a different interview with her, she brought up another song from the same Sondheim musical. She said, "Another song, called 'Every Day a Little Death,' has a similar tune to my song 'The World Spins.' The chords are similar. Sing it." When I interviewed Julee Cruise for *The Red Room Podcast* #157, she commanded me to sing "Every Day a Little Death" to prove her point. I had been preparing for this moment my entire life. A direct connection between *Twin Peaks* and Sondheim at the hands of Julee Cruise. Oh, you know I sang that song on the spot. I sang the song to and with

Julee Cruise. That is a moment I will never forget. I ended up beginning this book with a quote from "Every Day a Little Death" because of that Cruise moment and because it also connects to what Laura Palmer went through. The horror of being torn down each day. Piece by piece, her life force was attacked, but she kept fighting till the end. *FWWM* shows us her painful end. We knew she was going to die. We knew her dead before we knew her alive. But in the end she'll not have been dead when she dies. She lives forever as a hero to so many victims of sexual abuse and, for me, as someone who put on a positive face to the public while battling her demons from the inside and the out.

II.

Laura Palmer said, "I'll see you in twenty-five years. Meanwhile." I like to think *The Return* is the "I'll see you in twenty-five years" and *FWWM* is the "Meanwhile." *Twin Peaks* fans waited till 2017 for more of Cooper's story, but were given a feature film in 1992 about Laura Palmer. Up to the release of *FWWM*, TV viewers didn't have much information about who Laura Palmer was. She is in two flashbacks—a picnic in the pilot and a remembrance of her from James's perspective in Episode 1. All of her other appearances are contained in The Red Room, and an argument can be made as to whether that is truly Laura Palmer. This might be hard to remember in

My original copy of the diary
Photo by Scott Ryan

2022, but viewers and fans didn't have a lot of reasons to connect with Laura before *FWWM* was released.

Lynch was asked about his feelings for Laura Palmer/Sheryl Lee at the Cannes premiere in 1992. His comment, which is printed in *David Lynch Interviews*, edited by Richard A. Barney, was, "Sheryl Lee, who plays Laura Palmer, was hired to be a dead girl laying on a beach [actually a river bank]. It turns out, at least in my opinion, she's an unbelievable actress, and there are things that she's done in this movie that are truly incredible. I haven't seen too many people get into a role and give it as much. So the big news for me was this person hired to be a dead girl turns out to be a great actress and a perfect Laura Palmer."

The best place one could go for Laura Palmer content in 1990–1991 was a book written by Lynch's daughter Jennifer called *The Secret Diary of Laura Palmer*. This *New York Times* best seller had readers combing through the book for clues about the identity of her killer. The book takes readers from July 22, 1972, through February 24,1989, with some key pages ripped out. The pages that do survive help create one of the first arguments among fans about canon. One quick example: Laura makes an entry in the published diary on the day she dies, but in the film she gives her diary to Harold Smith a few days before her death. To be a fan of *Twin Peaks* is to let go of all the inconsistencies among the books, the series, the film, *The Return*, the trading cards, the lunch boxes, and the special-edition bicycle spokes. *The Secret Diary* is an amazing look into the suffering of Laura Palmer. As someone who read the book in 1990, I believe I was better prepared for the dark nature of *FWWM*. I had read about Laura's abuse, her sexual activity, and her desire to self-medicate, and once I heard that the film would revolve around her, I wasn't expecting a Disney-princess version of Laura. But because most casual ticket buyers didn't read the book before they saw the film, the average fan wasn't really expecting such a dark story. They wanted Cooper and they wanted their coffee and doughnuts. (Side note: There is not one doughnut in all of *FWWM*. But there is a gigantic helping of cocaine, with a side of countless scenes of sex with a minor.)

Expectations were a problem with every aspect of *Twin Peaks* since the debut of the pilot. Fans and critics reacted with disappointment to the Season 2 premiere, *FWWM*, and *The Return*. Everyone always wants what *they* think should happen in *Twin Peaks*, but every time Lynch gave them what he wanted. (Imagine the nerve of this guy.) Here is a great piece of advice if you want to be a true Lynch fan. Don't go into any Lynch project—painting, music, film, or television—with expectations. Let him serve you what he has prepared. Go in as blank as an empty canvas. He has his ideas, and he works hard to translate them to you in his own way . . . once he figures them out for himself.

During the writing, filming, and editing, *FWWM* was as fluid as black engine oil. Lynch wasn't quite sure what he wanted when he started, and he was still figuring it out right up through the editing process. Much of this will be discussed in Chapter 5 when I go over the various scripts, but it is also evident from the interviews conducted for the book. Lynch's ideas about the Angel, the ring, the use of original cast members, the meaning behind the Convenience Store, Agent Jeffries, and many other plot points were taking shape on the set and in editing. I am not alone in believing that *FWWM* was a piece of sculptable art while it was being crafted. *Twin Peaks* scholar John Thorne pioneered this thought when he came up with his theory that parts of *FWWM* are a dream. I won't go into his theory here because I don't want us to get sidetracked and I don't agree with it. Heck, after all these years, I'm not sure if John Thorne still believes in it. He wrote that in 2002 in *Wrapped in Plastic* #60, and a lot has changed since then. But the point is, you can see the film ebb and flow with conflicting ideas and content. It can be hard to pinpoint the whys and the hows because the film is very much in flux. That is part of the reason that it is so rewatchable. It leads in one direction and then changes, so each screening can take the viewer on a different path through the woods. This is one of Sheryl Lee's favorite parts. She told me in *The Blue Rose* #8, "This is the genius of David. If you take every single theory and walk it all the way to the end, then you are gonna hit a lot of obstacles in that theory."

As the managing editor of *The Blue Rose*, I have traveled to many *Twin Peaks* events over the years and interacted with thousands of fans. One of the things that truly shocked me the most in these interactions is the number of fans who have never seen *FWWM*. Part of the reason for this is that if a movie isn't streaming, it doesn't really exist in our current culture. For most of the past ten years, TOS has been available on just about every streaming platform; *FWWM* is rarely streaming anywhere for very long. Even fewer have seen the *Missing Pieces*, which are the collected deleted scenes from the film that Lynch edited together into one long feature for the 2014 box set. When I ask fans why they haven't seen it, they always say how much they love TOS and they just aren't really interested in the film. There are completists and then there are just casual fans. For us die-hards, it is hard to comprehend that point of view. On the flip side, there are a ton of fans who saw *FWWM* before the series, so that was their introduction to the world of *Twin Peaks*. It is a difficult fandom to wrap your mind around no matter which order you watched things in.

To those who have seen the original series but not the film, you are missing the very best part of *Twin Peaks*. I can't imagine skipping *FWWM* just because it wasn't on my play-next screen on Netflix or Hulu. I'm sure there are some of you out there who saw the film once and haven't seen it since, or you have just a passing memory of the times you have seen it. For you, not for those deadbeats who have never seen it, I will give you a quick recap of the film so that the rest of the book will make a little more sense. (Fun fact: I wrote the recap below from memory. Never even pulled up the film to double-check it. Superfans can skip to the next chapter.)

III.

The film begins with the static of a portable television set. The TV is smashed with an axe and the film is off and running. Teresa Banks (Pamela Gidley) is murdered. This was the murder that took place a year before Laura Palmer was killed. We never saw this character in the series, but Agent Cooper mentions her in the pilot episode. The first thirty-four minutes of the film are set in Deer Meadow, the inverse of Twin Peaks, where FBI Agents Chester Desmond (Chris Isaak) and Sam Stanley (Kiefer Sutherland) investigate the Banks murder. The sheriff (Gary Bullock) is not helpful, and the diner is staffed not by a smiling Norma, but by the more seasoned Irene, who does not appreciate jokes. The agents get their marching orders from FBI Regional Bureau Chief Gordon Cole (David Lynch) through clues from a woman dressed in a

This poster has hung in my house since 1992. Photo courtesy of New Line Cinema

red dress wearing a blue rose. This signifies a blue rose case, which will not be explained by Agent Desmond to Agent Stanley. We can infer it is a case that involves the supernatural world.

Desmond tangles with the sheriff, searches the victim's trailer, interviews a waitress at Hap's diner, and assists Stanley in the autopsy on Teresa Banks. As they prepare to leave, Desmond decides to take a trip back to Fat Trout Trailer Park, where Teresa lived. He is led to a trailer that is situated off by itself. He looks under the trailer and sees a mound of dirt with a green ring on top. As he reaches for the ring, the screen fades to black.

In Philadelphia, Agent Cooper (Kyle MacLachlan) enters Gordon Cole's office and tells him he is worried about a dream he had. This causes Cooper to keep checking the surveillance cameras. While he does this, long-lost FBI Agent Phillip Jeffries (David Bowie) appears and tells Cooper, Cole, and Albert Rosenfield (Miguel Ferrer) that he is not gonna talk about Judy, asks if they know who Cooper is, and says he has been to one of "their" meetings. Static fills the screen as we fade to what is called The Room Above the Convenience Store (TRATCS). We see the evil spirit Bob (Frank Silva) talking with the Man From Another Place (Michael J. Anderson) at a Formica table. The room is populated by strange characters including an old woman (Frances Bay) and her grandson (Jonny Leppell). As Jeffries starts screaming with pain, he disappears from the FBI office and Albert finds out that Desmond has disappeared from Deer Meadow.

Agent Cooper heads to Deer Meadow and studies the trailer park, but finds the case cold and wonders when the killer will strike again. "ONE YEAR LATER" appears on the screen, and Laura Palmer (Sheryl Lee) walks down the street with her friends as they head to high school. She starts the school day off with a line of cocaine in the bathroom, meets James (James Marshall) for a sexual rendezvous, then chats with Donna (Moira Kelly) after school about boys. Upon arriving back at her house, Laura looks through her secret diary and realizes that pages have been torn out. She takes the diary to Harold Smith (Lenny Von Dohlen), a shut-in whom she met through her Meals on Wheels route, and tells him Bob ripped the pages out and wants to kill her. She leaves the diary with him.

She heads to the Double R Diner to pick up her Meals on Wheels deliveries. (Hey, I just realized she should have done this before going to Harold's to save on gas, since she had to go back to his house to deliver a meal.) The old woman and her grandson from earlier show up and give Laura a painting and tell her that the man behind the mask is looking for the book with the pages torn out. She heads home and goes to her hiding place for the diary, only to see Bob standing there. She runs out of the house and hides under a bush in the neighbor's yard and sees her father (Ray Wise) come out of the house. She can't conceive that her father is Bob, the demon who has been molesting her since she was a child. She runs to Donna sobbing and asks Donna if she is her friend.

Back home, she has dinner with her parents. Her father yells at her to wash her hands and wants to know who her secret lover is. Leland sits on the edge of his bed and Bob leaves him. He cries and goes to Laura's room, telling her that he loves her. She goes to sleep with the painting on her wall. She ends up inside the painting, where Agent Cooper tells her to not take the ring, the same ring that Teresa Banks wore. She sees Annie Blackburn (Heather Graham) in bed with her. Annie says, "The good Dale is in the lodge and he can't leave. Write it in your diary." Laura looks away and Annie disappears. The ring is in Laura's palm. She awakens, and the ring is gone.

Laura spends a wild night at a bar in Canada with Jacques Renault, Donna, and two johns. The music is so loud that their dialogue can be understood only by the subtitles on the screen. Laura runs into Ronette Pulaski (Phoebe Augustine) and parties with her. Leland picks Laura up in the morning from Donna's house, and the One-Armed Man (Al Strobel) chases them in his car. He yells to Laura, "It is your father," but she can't hear him over the loud engine. She asks her father if he came home the other day; he says he did. But this still isn't enough for her to believe the unbelievable. That night, Laura knows Bob will come to visit her. He climbs through her window; she stays lucid and tries to really see who it is who has been raping her for so many years. She sees for the first time that it is her father. She screams.

The following morning she tells her father to stay away from her, and he knows what he must do. That evening he follows her as she runs off with James and then heads to a cabin with Leo Johnson (Eric Da Re), Jacques, and Ronette. Leland enters once the men are gone, takes the girls to a train car, punches Ronette, and ties up Laura. He and Bob try to persuade her to let Bob inhabit her. She refuses. The OAM shows up and throws the ring into the train car. Laura puts it on and is murdered. Leland wraps her in plastic and heads to the entrance of The Red Room. Bob, MFAP, and OAM talk and remove the blood and garmonbozia (pain and suffering) from Leland. Elsewhere in The Red Room, Laura is sitting with Agent Cooper at her side. An angel appears above her, a light shines on her face, and she laughs and cries, experiencing true happiness for the first time in her life.

CHAPTER 3

One of Their Meetings

Over the years, I have had the opportunity to conduct some amazing interviews with the cast of *Twin Peaks*, whether for *The Red Room Podcast*, *The Blue Rose* magazine, my documentary called *Voyage to Twin Peaks*, or *The Harold Smith Stay In/Play In* Facebook event. I have been fortunate enough to travel with Mike McGraner's *FWWM* tour. He shows the film and then offers a Q and A with cast members. I also published the *Twin Peaks Unwrapped* podcast's book through the *Blue Rose* company, and Ben Durant and Bryon Kozaczka talked to just about everyone for their book. Finally, I've published a few Lynch books, *Conversations with Mark Frost* and *The Women of David Lynch*, through Fayetteville Mafia Press, which I run with David Bushman. I have been lucky enough to interview almost everyone. This chapter compiles comments about the film from all those projects in one place. This isn't quite an oral history, but these are quotes from the participants of *FWWM* gathered together for "one of their meetings."

Robert Engels (cowriter of *FWWM*): By the time the second season was ending, David and I had become pretty good friends. He asked me if I would like to write with him. I was over at David's house, and he said, "I just talked with the French, and we are going to do a *Twin Peaks* movie." And we just started it right then. (*BRM*)

Mark Frost (cocreator of *Twin Peaks*): I was busy doing *Storyville*, and given where we ended, how we'd left the audience at the end of the series, I thought it was an opportunity to go forward and tell more of the story rather than backward and go over what felt to me like familiar ground. It was predominantly that I didn't have the bandwidth at that moment. I was up to my eyebrows. If it had been my choice alone, I would not have gone that way. Lynch felt strongly this was the film he wanted to make, so I said, "By all means, go ahead." (*CWMF*)

Sheryl Lee (Laura Palmer): I don't remember when I read the script. Because I remember having creative conversations with David about the film, I knew her last seven days were going to be included in the story. We would have a lot of creative discussions about it, so I feel like by the time I read a script, I already had a sense of what the story was going to be. (Mike McGraner's *FWWM* tour)

Mike Malone (set dresser): David only took three crew members from the TV show to work on *FWWM*: Laurie Hudson, the wardrobe girl; Cori Glazer, the script supervisor; and me, the set dresser. We were shooting the scene with the bus. I whispered in Cori's ear, "Looks like Chris Isaak could use some help." She knew what I meant. She said to David, "I think there should be some more agents out there?" Lynch says, "Malone, Huck, you're in the FBI!" Jon Huck was our sound mixer. We go off to wardrobe. I put on one of Kyle MacLachlan's suits. David put us out there, and the rest is history. Five days before shooting started on *FWWM*, I was playing basketball with a lot of the cast members. We were going for a loose ball and my hand went straight into Dana Ashbrook's chest. I broke a bone in the back of my hand. So I had a cast on my hand, and I almost didn't get to be the set dresser because I had to convince them I could do it with a cast on my hand. If you look at the movie, you will see that on my left hand is a cast. You can see my gun at the end of my hand. (*BRM*)

Mike Malone can be seen wearing a cast in this shot.
Photo courtesy of New Line Cinema

Gary Bullock (Sheriff Cable): I thought of Sheriff Cable as being unhinged. He is so strong that he could bend a piece of steel rebar, and he is up against a guy who is smaller in size, but when he fights, he's just a thug. So when he gets flummoxed by this guy, he goes berserk. David wanted the fight to be loose, and just go nuts. I look at the scene now, and I wish we had more time. The picture of me bending steel was the first thing we did. We had to get a bent piece of rebar, and no one could bend it. So they took a truck with a lift on it, and that is how they bent it. It was heavy as hell. The stuff we used in the scene was fake, and anyone could bend it. (*RRP*)

THE CONVENIENCE STORE

John Neff (sound mixer on *FWWM* Blu-ray release): David is a very hands-on guy in sound. He believes that sound is half of the picture. He will say, "It has to sound like it's in a stone canyon." Then it is up to me to make it sound like that. When he uses the war whoop from the Man From Another Place in *FWWM*, he will use that as a clue to take you in the right direction. (*RRP*)

Robert Engels: The Formica table is really important. There were these ants under it, and then in another room was a television, and Eisenhower's inauguration was on TV. We hit on that because we were talking about how the inauguration was in the evening for people on the West Coast, and it was delayed a half hour because it was the same day that on *I Love Lucy* that Lucy had her baby—which was the most watched episode at the time. That is how we got to Eisenhower playing on TV. That is how convoluted we got. It was nuts. It plays with the thing that there are different times and realities going on. It's all pretty dreamy. So that table is important. That was in one of the drafts. Then we got rid of it. (*BRM*)

Mike Malone: I think David thought, "This is what I want, a four-hour version." But you can't release that version. He shot what he wanted to shoot. I forgot about the scene with Phillip Jeffries showing up on the stairs and the guy shitting his pants. We cracked up about that for days. That was just a crew rallying cry. Anytime you wanted to make one of the crew laugh, you just say, "The shit-a-come out of my pants." Then you go see it in the theater and you are like, "What happened to that scene?" (*BRM*)

Jonny Leppell (Mrs. Tremond's grandson): I filmed the Black Lodge scene down in LA. Bob was the only scene that ever gave me nightmares. I didn't even know what was going on because I was ten years old at the time. They filmed everything backward, and they had an optic camera that went down our throats when we said "Electricity." Frances Bay (Mrs. Tremond) took me under her wing. (*VTTP*)

Mona Leppell (mother of child actor Jonny Leppell): There are a little bit of risqué scenes. Jonny never saw any of that. He mainly shot with Frances Bay and Sheryl Lee, and their scenes were perfectly normal. They hired him on the spot. He did his first scene that night, where he jumped through the mud puddle. (*VTTP*)

Jonny Leppell: They needed someone to fill in for David Lynch's son, who was going to be absent during the scene. I went up to David, who was in his director's chair. There were two other kids. He asked me to jump like a bunny rabbit. He asked me to do it three times in a row. He said, "Perfect." I got a haircut, and they fitted me for a mask, which didn't have any eyeholes in it. We filmed the first scene. I was just going to wear the mask and do the scene where Ray Wise comes out of the hotel. (*VTTP*)

Mona Leppell: He was just gonna be a double for David Lynch's son. When he first shot in North Bend, he had the mask on. He got to speak, but you didn't see his face. We assumed that was his role; he was never gonna be seen. Three weeks went by and we got another call, and they asked if he could come to LA and shoot with Frances Bay. (*VTTP*)

TRAIN CAR

Ray Wise (Leland Palmer): I remember that crazy night. It was probably two thirty in the morning, and we're out in the woods with these old train cars on this old track that is long forgotten. It was cold and dark and I had a flashlight, and I had David Lynch yelling at me, "All right, Ray, keep it moving, Ray. Keep it moving, Ray." It was all challenging, really. (Mike McGraner's *FWWM* tour)

Mike Malone: It was the last week of Laura's life, and it wasn't a pleasant week. Sheryl has to do a scene being dragged into a train car. She isn't gonna joke around with you before the shot. She was so down the entire movie. Her character was down, and she had to be down as well. (*BRM*)

SHERYL LEE

Al Strobel (The One-Armed Man): After the day's shoot, we got back to the hotel, and Sheryl Lee was still really upset. She was shaking and everything. My significant other was with me. She is a spiritual counselor and got Sheryl in the hotel room and gave her a bit of a gentle massage and swept up the whole room with juniper smoke, and that cleans the air. She got Sheryl pretty well calmed down. It was an intense day. (*BRM*)

Lenny Von Dohlen (Harold Smith): It was heaven to work with Sheryl Lee. It was the bravest performance I have seen of any of her contemporaries. In that movie, she just bared it all for the role, for David, and for all time. I think she is superb, and a credit to our profession, and one of the nicest people there is. (FBL)

Mike Malone: It was just a lot of Sheryl Lee in the woods screaming her head off. She is such a nice gal, and to see her get tortured for a couple of months out in the woods was just a downer. Everyone likes her and thinks she is great, but seeing her screaming all week . . . man. (*BRM*)

Sheryl Lee: As fun as working with David is, acting in those types of roles is extremely lonely. To this day [pauses for a beat] there might be only one person that I have truly talked to about what it was like to play that character. It was so private and personal. In order to be able to hold that focus and contain that emotional vase for that time, it takes just such fine-tuning. Otherwise it won't work. You won't have any more tears left, or you will go too far and won't be able to come back. There is an edge sometimes where actors can . . . you know when you get tired; the veils become thinner. Good directors like David understand how to watch for the signs and take care of their actors. (*BRM*)

Dana Ashbrook (Bobby Briggs): I will always love the scene with Sheryl where Laura and Bobby are in the woods and they are trying to make the drug deal with the cop. That whole sequence was just a special night. It was super-freezing cold, and we were out in the woods, and it was a long scene, a very long scene. Sheryl Lee was amazing in it. She was so good; when we got to that point in the scene where she was so annoying and I just couldn't make her do anything, it was so much fun. It was a great night for me. I loved doing it. David was right there with us. He was in the trenches with us. He got in there and put on some rubber gloves and was arranging the brains on the cop's head. It was three o'clock in the morning, and Sheryl and I would start the scene *way* off in the woods, and [Lynch called] "Action!" They couldn't even see us or hear us, and finally we would get to the place where the scene would start. It was crazy. We were just pretending to be crazy kids. (*BRM*)

Sheryl Lee is tormented by Ray Wise in a scene from *FWWM*.
Photo courtesy of New Line Cinema

Robert Engels: She was great. I guess you could say that was a gamble, but if you know her you knew she could do it. The great thing about Sheryl is that she was fearless, just fearless. That is a really great thing for an actor. "Could she pull this off?" was never a question, because you knew she'll do it, and David will help. The movie had to be about her. David is so great. Actors just adore him. They will go through brick walls for him. (*BRM*)

Ray Wise: She just went through hell making that film—just performed beautifully. She ran the gamut of every conceivable human emotion and did it so beautifully. Words escape me when I talk about her performance in the film. I was present for a lot of it. Some of the moments we had together are some of my favorite ones. (*BRM*)

Sheryl Lee: Ray is a genius. He and Grace [Zabriskie], they leave me speechless. That fast—boom!—they can switch from hysterically funny to some of the deepest soulful drama to the scariest spine-chilling look. Just a look, and it terrifies you. Their range as actors is unbelievable. They are geniuses. They both are the kindest—wonderful people to be around. (*BRM*)

BOB

Ray Wise: I never equated myself with Bob. I always felt that no matter what I did as the character, it was always Leland. As an actor, I never felt that I was Frank Silva's character in any way. *Ever.* I felt it was Leland. Whether he was two beings in the same person, I don't know. I always felt there was an evil Leland and a good Leland. It is interesting [pause] now that I am talking about it [pause] it is very strange. When I look in the mirror in the series, you saw Bob, but I saw only Leland. It was just two different sides of the same coin. I think there is good and bad in everyone. They are not always possessed by a Bob, but as we find out when Leland is lying under the water in Cooper's arms, and Cooper is reciting the Tibetan Book of the Dead, we find out that it is a revelation to Leland that he did all those bad things. But as an actor, I always felt that I was Leland and never even thought about Bob, actually. (*BRM*)

CAMPER

Al Strobel: I scared the shit out of David when I was stunt driving. Ray was in the Cadillac convertible, and I started having fun with my little camper. I even got it up on two wheels at one point. He was on the walkie-talkie with me, and I could tell I scared him. And then we did the scene where I stopped the camper close to the Palmers' car. I think it was done in one take. David asked me to rev the car a couple of times, and he had a couple of grips jump up and down on the back bumper. So my camper was rocking up and down. And he said, "Don't worry about being heard above all this noise, because we can always dub back in in post." Using all my techniques, I was able to be understood well enough above all the ruckus that we didn't have to dub it in. My focus during that scene is on Laura, because I want to tell her she is driving with a murderer and a rapist. I shouted past Ray because he was in the driver's seat. I could tell out of the corner of my eye that he was kind of spooked too. (*BRM*)

One of the lines from this scene has become a fan favorite.
Photo courtesy of New Line Cinema

"THIS IS WHERE WE LIVE, SHELLY"

Robert Engels: That line is David. I can remember writing the scene, because we were at his house. I would type, and I remember him saying, "This is where we live, Shelly," and we laughed about it. It is perfect Leo stuff. (*BRM*)

Mädchen Amick (Shelly): Out of all the things that I was involved in, "This is where we live, Shelly," boy, does that say a lot in one line. I always see that. I didn't know it would be so popular. I love it, though. (*WOL*)

LEGACY

Ray Wise: In my mind, now, I consider it David's masterpiece. That's the way I feel about it. And for my money, the last twenty minutes of this movie is almost like a religious experience. If I were to have one. (Mike McGraner's *FWWM* tour)

Sheryl Lee: I've only seen the film one time since it came out originally. So I only saw it again before we went back to shoot *The Return*; I rewatched everything. But speaking of religious experiences, I am very, very grateful that Laura got an angel at the end, for sure. (Mike McGraner's *FWWM* tour)

Moira Kelly (Donna Hayward): When I was cast in *FWWM*, I was psyched and sick to my stomach. It was the same feeling you get when you're the new kid at school. You're coming in as an outsider. This was a cast and crew that had been working together for years and a character established by another actress. So I was a bit nervous. But from the first day, I felt right at home. David infused the set with comfort and freedom to explore without inhibition. (*TPU* book)

Lenny Von Dohlen: Sheryl and I were called to the set around 2:00 p.m., and by the time we actually got on the set it was 3:00 a.m. That is a long time to stay on simmer. We both knew what the job was, and we helped each other. Then we let the floodgates break. David Lynch screamed across the sound stage, "Deepak [Nayar, first assistant director], never schedule the most important scene in the movie for 3:00 a.m.!" That's a canny director getting two tired actors hyped up and focused. At the end, I remember seeing something in the corner of my eye, and I looked, and it was David doing this leprechaun version of a jig. He is taking a moment that something happened and celebrating it and moving on to the next scene, because there was another scene to do. He is a very special man to make all that happen in the first place and then to celebrate it. (FBL)

Al Strobel: The critics actually really got it all wrong, as it has been proved by time. Time has actually shown that it was a great movie. And the critics simply did not understand it. I think it's going to last forever. And hey, in the end I got to work with David Lynch, for God's sake! (*BRM*)

Sheryl Lee: Even though it was challenging. I was with the best of the best. Even the most grueling days were that way for a bigger reason. I never was thinking, "I hate this. Why am I doing it?" I loved every second of it. I loved the exhaustion of it. The way David filmed it, once I was in it, I was in it. I wouldn't have changed anything about that. He wrote a story that was brutal for this character—as it is for so many real-life victims. (*BRM*)

Dana Ashbrook: I think it's a great movie. Some of my favorite scenes are in that movie. Again, it's David Lynch, man! If you keep looking at it, the film can become different things. Especially with the new *Twin Peaks*, you revisit [*FWWM*] and you start to understand things a little more. Or see things differently. Like any piece of art that is out there for a while, you notice different things. The fact that people are talking about it after all these years is indicative of the minds of David Lynch and Mark Frost. (*BRM*)

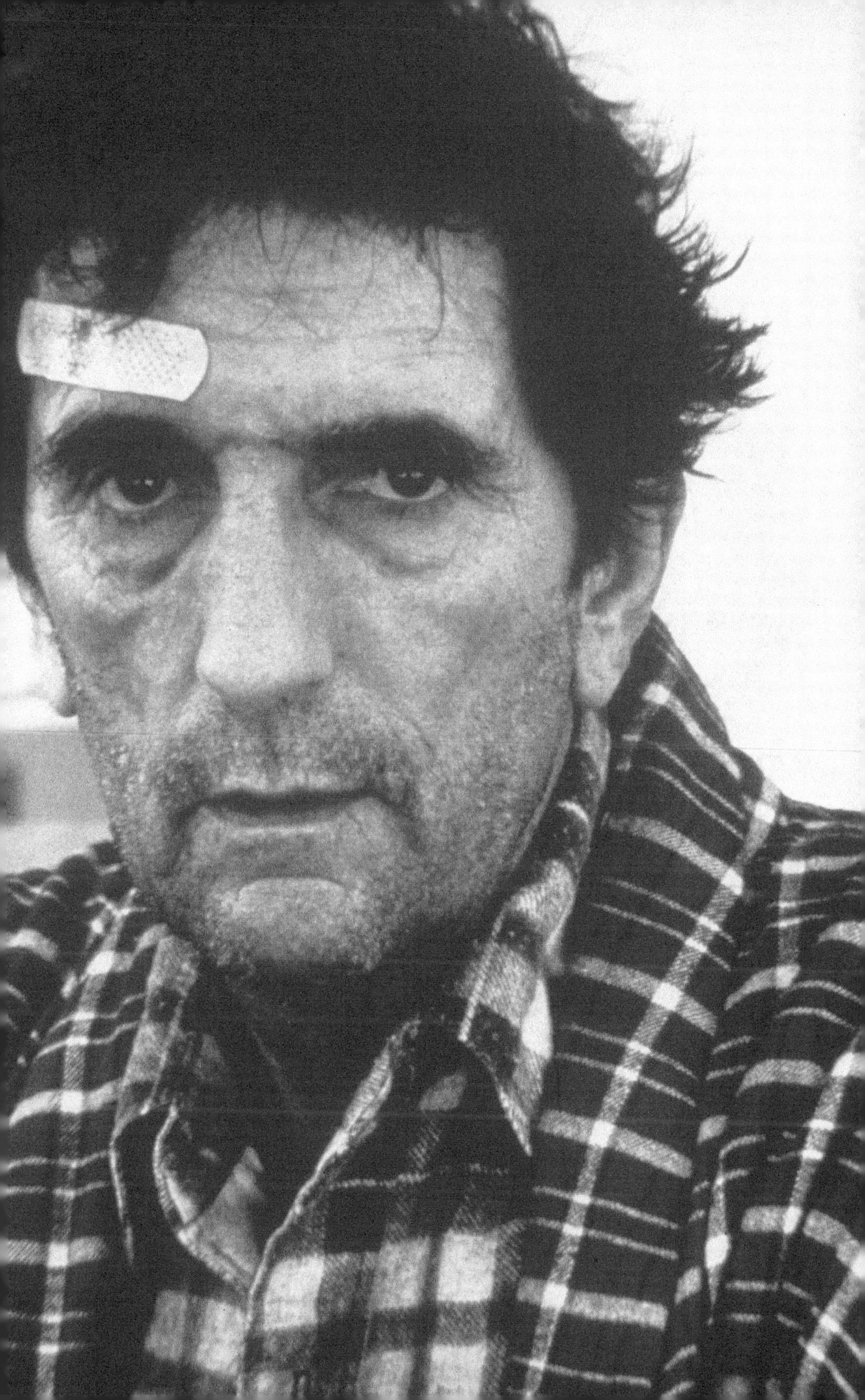

CHAPTER 4

It's Your Producer, Gregg Fiendberg

The original poster for *FWWM* has hung beside my computer, no matter where I have lived, since I bought it at Spencer's Gifts in 1992. While working on the book, I often turn to my left to make sure I am spelling someone's name right. As I was looking at the poster, one name popped out at me: Gregg Fienberg. Why had I never interviewed him? That night, I watched an episode of *Deadwood*, and there was his name again. This guy was following me. In looking at his IMDB listing, I saw he also produced *Big Little Lies*, *Sharp Objects*, and *True Blood* and worked with Madonna on *Truth or Dare*. I was disheartened. If he knew Madonna, why would he do an interview with me about a film he produced thirty years ago? Never underestimate the power of working with David Lynch and having worked on something as momentous as *Twin Peaks*. Gregg Fienberg didn't produce just the film, he also produced Seasons 1 and 2 of the series. Luckily for all of us, he wanted to look back on one of his earlier production jobs. I'm thankful for this interview, because all of his stories were completely new to me, and that was a big treat.

Scott Ryan: How did *Twin Peaks* come into your life?

Gregg Fienberg: You know this was a long time ago, right? [Laughs.] I was working at Propaganda Films. They were involved with the pilot of *Twin Peaks.* I had done U2's *Rattle and Hum*, so I was one of the people who had longer-term experience. I was this young kid. They had an issue with the producer on the pilot, and I got nominated to do the series.

Ryan: Do you remember how you found out who killed Laura Palmer?

Fienberg: [Thinks for a beat.] No. [Laughs.] I remember along the way we knew about Killer Bob. I think when that script came out is when I found out who it was once and for all. I was getting inklings along the way. Anyone who says they knew all along, I wouldn't accept that answer unless it was David Lynch or Mark Frost. My recollection is they didn't even have it up their sleeves from the beginning, but they would be the only two that could have known.

Ryan: How did you get to be the producer on *FWWM*?

Fienberg: I will tell you exactly how the movie came to be. I know this story better than anybody. We had a book deal. It was for four books. We had done three of them already [*The Secret Diary of Laura Palmer*; *The Autobiography of F.B.I. Special Agent Dale Cooper: My Life, My Tapes*; and *Welcome to Twin Peaks: An Access Guide to the Town*]. I was very tight with one of the creative people at ABC, who was filling me in on everything and what was going to happen with the series. We knew it was going to get canceled. The day ABC officially canceled the series, we knew that meant everything was done, including the book deal. It was depressing. That night at two in the morning, I was thinking about what had befallen us. I suddenly had this idea. The fourth book should be the continuation of *Twin Peaks*—what the third season would have been if the show had been picked up. Then I thought, *Wait a minute, forget the fourth book—let's do the third season as a movie.* This was back before movies were being made from TV shows. In the middle of the night, I am like, *Oh my God, we are gonna make a movie of this thing!*

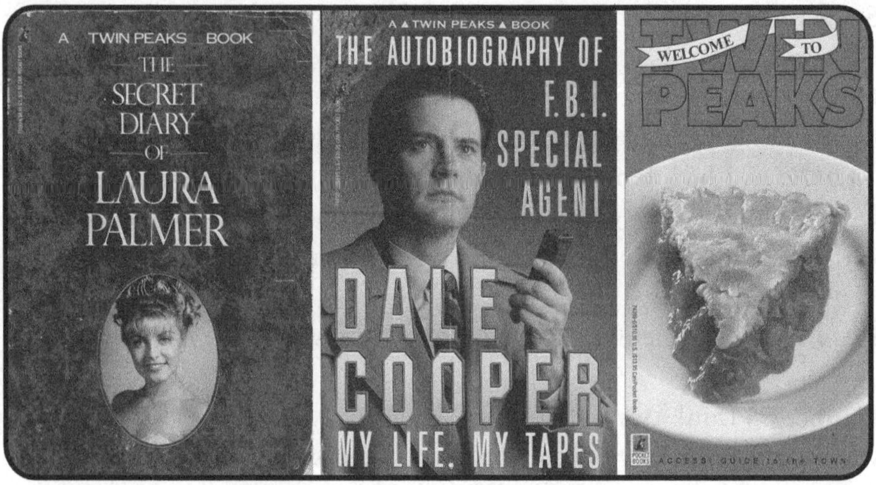

The three books that were released during the original run.
Photo by Scott Ryan

I got up at seven in the morning. I called Tony Krantz, who was David and Mark's agent. I said, "Tony, you are gonna think I am crazy, but why don't we do a movie of the third season?" He said, "That's a crazy good idea. I'm calling David." I think I had some idea that another person would be found dead, or some silly idea. Tony called me back an hour later and said, "I talked to David. He loves the idea, but he doesn't want to do a sequel; he wants to do a prequel. He wants to show everything that led up to before Laura was dead. I am gonna see what I can do. I'm going to call a French financier who wants to work with David." And I kid you not, by noon we had a greenlit movie.

Ryan: Really, that fast?

Fienberg: Later that day Tony was like, "David's on board, Mark's on board, we are gonna make a movie." That was it.

Ryan: And do you remember what month this was?

Fienberg: Whatever day the news came out that *Twin Peaks* was canceled, it was the next day. [*Twin Peaks* was canceled by ABC on May 22, 1991.] I am a producer, and I have to figure out what we need, but we had all the sets. For all intents and purposes, we had what we needed. So if we were gonna do it, now was the time. Things had to get figured out, and deals had to be made, but my recollection is it was a 7:00 a.m. call, and by noon it was greenlit. Most people don't know that story, but that is how it happened.

Ryan: What were your responsibilities on *FWWM*?

Fienberg: At the time, I was a line producer; now I am more of a creative executive producer. I made the trains run on time, basically.

Ryan: Were you concerned about the length of the script? Did you think the film would be too long?

Fienberg: I do remember when the script came in, and we only had so much money. David is a genius director; he can figure out anything. After shooting the series, we knew how pages to minutes were converted. I said to David, "If we shoot this entire script, it's probably going to come out at five hours long." He said, "No, it won't." The first cut was at least five hours. So that is a lot of footage to shoot in forty-six days. But if the director decides he is gonna get that done, then we have to get it done. I'm sure we had a lot of long days.

Ryan: How was it to film in the Snoqualmie area? It's so beautiful there.

Fienberg: We were there for a couple weeks, and you know it is constantly raining in the Seattle area, and I don't think it ever rained once for our entire shoot. We left and came back to LA to shoot that portion, and then the next week Seattle had an ice storm that was like headline news because of trees breaking in half and traffic accidents. I remember feeling that we had great luck and were meant to make that movie at that time.

Ryan: Sheryl Lee gives an incredible performance. What do you remember about watching her develop that character on film?

Fienberg: I have memories of us having to make sure she was OK on a day-to-day basis. I don't think we had to shut down because of it, but I recall us having to schedule around some of the exhaustion she was experiencing because her performance was so incredible and so intense. We had to make sure she had time to recuperate.

Ryan: What did you think about the rest of the *Twin Peaks* television series cast being cut out of the film and it focusing on the Laura Palmer story?

Fienberg: When I first heard David wanted to do the prequel, my first thought was disappointment, because I thought I came up with a great idea to make Season 3 as a movie, but then I thought, *Of course! That's why he's David.* That's genius, because I am far more interested in that than I am in the sequel, because I am invested in these people. Laura's story was the true story. Who was Laura Palmer? I thought it was a great idea. From the moment we got going it was like, *Let's do this. Fans are gonna love it.*

Ryan: Any stories from working with David Bowie in the film?

Fienberg: We went out to a cast dinner two days before we started

Even David Bowie didn't understand who he was in the film, but David Lynch wasn't about to explain it—all part of being on the Blue Rose Task Force. Photo courtesy of New Line Cinema

shooting. We were in a private room at a really nice restaurant. It was a giant conversation with everybody around the table, and Bowie said to David, "I have a question for you. So my character kind of pops in, and can you at least give me a clue as to who my character is and what the hell he is doing there?" David says, "NO, I CAN'T!" And we all busted out laughing. And Bowie is like, "OK." David said, "I'll take care of you." Bowie asked the question we were all wondering. It was so well delivered from David, and a brilliant moment.

Ryan: How did you feel about the reception of the film?

Fienberg: This gets into a creative discussion. The unfortunate thing is that when you have a five-hour movie that you cut down to under two and half hours, there is going to be a lot of story that you miss. Anytime I am developing a project with writers, I would rather figure out how to tell the story in two and a half hours really well, and if it needs to be five hours, then we have a problem. I think that is what happened. It might have been better to figure that out in the script phase, but David is David, and he has his ideas. In today's era, we would have done a limited series to finish out the show and maybe a network would have let us do a six-hour finish. But back then, that beast didn't exist. No one even considered that.

I think that was part of the issue: you had a story that was not easy to understand and had a lot of mystery to it. When you have a series that was as popular as Season 1 was, and then Season 2 the rating dipped and people weren't responding to it as much, and then you do a movie that was even more hard to follow than the second season, maybe that was what happened.

Ryan: Have you noticed the reassessment of *FWWM*?

Fienberg: People I work with are always amazed that I did the original *Twin Peaks*. Now that I have been doing this for as long as I have, I used to be one of the youngest people on the set and now I am one of the oldest, but a lot of young people want to come up to me and talk about *Twin Peaks* and the movie. I do think that what that speaks to is that it was such a groundbreaking TV show, especially in Season 1. When the movie came out, they wanted it to be that great thing it was in Season 1, and David is an artist. He does things the way he wants to do them. People have to think about that when they are watching his projects. It's not easy to just sit back and dig in and watch. I think at the time there was a rawness around the whole show and the expectation of it. Now people are over that, and they can sit back and just watch it for what it is and then it seeps in. When you watch it that way, you realize how brilliant it is. David is beyond a brilliant director in what he can get actors to do. I still, till this day, and I have worked with some great directors, haven't seen anyone else be able to do what he does.

Ryan: What did you take with you from *Twin Peaks* to help with the rest of your career?

Fienberg: I remember a lot about the creative process of that show. Some of it positive and some of it negative. I have my own feelings about doing the second season and where it was going while we were making it.

Ryan: Tell me about that. What went wrong in Season 2?

Fienberg: There was something. I am not sure I can explain where I feel it went wrong. The best way I can describe it is that in the first season, when those scripts came in, everyone would get together and we wouldn't talk about *how* we were going to make it. We would just talk about the scripts. The crew was the first people who got to see those scripts. And we were saying to each other, "What do you think this means? What does the red dress mean?" We didn't care how we were gonna shoot any of it. If it was too long, too short, too expensive, we didn't care. We were just totally engrossed. It was like a book club, and everyone would get together and freak out about this brilliant script all the way through the first season, and it started out that way in the second season.

Then, after the killer of Laura Palmer was revealed, which was wrongly forced upon David and Mark by the network, we weren't talking about the scripts anymore. I remember people from the art department coming into my office and saying, "We don't even understand what we are supposed to do. Can you help us?" I would have to go to the writers and say, "What exactly is happening, because we have to do continuity with the sets and someone has to build something and we don't even know what it is?" At that point, I went to the writers about it and they said, "No, it's all fine," but my gut felt it wasn't all fine, and it turned out it wasn't all fine. The audience speaks with the ratings.

Ryan: People always beat up on Season 2, but there still are some pretty damn fine episodes.

Fienberg: There was great stuff, but when you have fire like that you've got to keep it. I have had that experience, and everyone I have worked with since knows I've had that experience. I guess, for me, I've been on multiple shows since where if I am getting that inkling—and now I work much closer with writers than I did back then—I can influence shows more now because they certainly know I have experience with it. So if my gut is screaming we are having a problem, I have taken that with me because I vowed on any other show that I worked that I would speak up well in advance if I felt I was losing the crew. I can always tell if my crew is into a show or not. If they don't get it, then probably the audience won't either. Now I am not sure if on *Twin Peaks* I would have been able to have an influence . . .

Ryan: You would not have.

Fienberg: . . . based on the creative people involved, like David. And that is OK too. If that is what David and Mark wanted to do, then hopefully we helped them execute it to the best of our ability. And as you say, it was still pretty damn good. Nobody ever stopped trying, that is for sure—all the way to the end.

Ryan: I have to thank you for *Deadwood.*

Fienberg: Thank you very much. Part of what I took away from *Twin Peaks* is built deeply into *Deadwood.* That was a scenario where I worked very closely with David Milch and actually had that relationship with him where I could talk through things and hopefully influence things, not that Milch needed much. That was a special one for sure.

Ryan: You've worked with some amazing people in your career. What is your strongest memory about working on *FWWM*?

Fienberg: Well, I am up in the office and the first AD says, "David wants to talk to you on the walkie." And David never wanted to talk to me on the walkie-talkie. So David says, "Gregg, let me tell you what I am gonna need next. I don't need it today, but I am going to need it tomorrow." I said, "OK, what is it?" He said, "What I am going to need tomorrow is a pig's fetus." And I'm like, "A pig's fetus?" He says, "Yes, I have an idea for something. I am not gonna tell you what it is. Can you see if there is any way we can have a pig's fetus tomorrow?" I said, "Sure." So I had the production team call Pierce College, which is in Los Angeles and is an animal college. They didn't have one, but they said to call a university in the Midwest in farming country. They called that university, and this sums up what we do in production: in like ten minutes my team came back to me and said, "Does David want a pink one or a black one?" So I called David on the walkie and asked, "Would you like a pink one or a black one?" And he said, "ONE OF EACH!" [Laughs.] I said, "It'll be here in the morning." He used them with something with Laura where she pokes something. That is a moment I will never forget.

Ryan: I don't remember a pig's fetus in the movie.

Fienberg: I'd have to look through and see if I could find where it is. But the way he used it, it was used to replicate human skin, if I recall. It wasn't like you would know it was a pig's fetus; it was used in another way. But that is what he needed, and it definitely got used.

Ryan: And that is how you get your other producing jobs. You just tell them, "If someone needs a pig's fetus, I'm your guy." And then you get hired.

Fienberg: That's right. That's how I got *Deadwood*.

CHAPTER 5

Write It in Your Script

A FREAK ACCIDENT

There really wasn't anything going on in the midnineties for *Twin Peaks* fans. Once *FWWM* was released on VHS for rental, that pretty much ended it. The film came and went with a whimper. It disappeared like Chet Desmond in a trailer park. So it was a complete surprise to me when I was used-CD shopping and the proprietor was talking to a customer about how that very morning someone dropped off the shooting script for *FWWM* and he had it in his possession. When he mentioned there were scenes that were not in the final movie, I leaped higher than the Jumping Man. I didn't know either of the people who were talking, but you can bet I immediately butted in with "Can I see the script?" The longhaired, scary owner, who totally could have been cast as one of the guys working on the lamps outside Hap's Diner, looked at me for a second. He sized up the tall, skinny, twentysomething who had Kramer hair. He tossed a manila envelope on top of the Broadway CDs I was perusing.

I pulled out the title page:

Twin Peaks
FIRE WALK WITH ME
Teresa Banks and the Last Seven Days of Laura Palmer
By David Lynch
and Robert Engels

CONFIDENTIAL
August 8th, 1991

It might have said "Confidential," but I read that as For Scott's Eyes Only. I flipped through the loose pages and saw the names Ben Horne, Nadine Hurley, Pete Martell, Lucy Moran—they were all there. I was skimming a *Twin Peaks* item that was *new* to me. The store was not very big. In fact, no matter how small you imagine the store was, it was three times smaller than that. You were always about five steps away from the door. I really wanted to purchase that mint double disk *Miss Saigon* original-cast album, but I also knew there was no way I was leaving that store without this script. Steal it or ask for it? Hmmm. WWCD?

This might be a good place for a confession. I have committed only one count of larceny in my life, and it was all for *Twin Peaks*. Back in 1993 when *FWWM* came out on video, I was working at a video store. At that time when movies were released on VHS, the cost for one movie was over one hundred dollars. With my employee discount, it would cost me eighty dollars, which was more than I made in a week. I had just graduated college and had no job prospects. Spending a week of my paycheck on the VHS of *FWWM* wasn't in the cards for me. But not owning it wasn't a satisfying solution for me either. So here, in print, I freely admit for the first time that I stole that videocassette the day it came out. No renter ever got their "Be Kind Rewind" hands on one of the three copies my store purchased. Two for them. One for me. I quit the store a few weeks later. If the Massillon police want to come lock me up, I hope I at least get to see a vision of Louise Dombrowski doing the flashlight dance as I rot in my cell for this high crime. As for the royalties to Frost/Lynch, I am pretty damn sure I made it up with the action figures, Funko flunkos, and subpar Showtime apparel purchases I have made over the years.

The point is, I had stolen once before for *FWWM*, and I was prepared to do it again. I thought that before I commit crime number two and start down the path of Hank Jennings, maybe I should ask, "Sir, can I please take this to the Kinko's up the street and photocopy it? I will leave my driver's license here as collateral. But I am a huge *Twin Peaks* fan, and I just need to have this."

You have to remember, there was no internet to speak of in 1995. There was no quest for the *Missing Pieces*—there were no known pieces to miss. You couldn't just Google the script, which is now available at the flick of our fingers. In fact, in 1995 I didn't know anyone who gave a puked-up pile of garmonbozia about *Twin Peaks*. The fact that I was at that store on the exact day he happened to stumble across this script in a small town in Ohio is still the luckiest coincidence that has ever happened to me. My hands grasped the manila envelope while I eyed the door to see if I could bum-rush the lady by the classical CDs to make my escape. Hap's lighting man said, "Sure, kid, I trust you." I bought the *Miss Saigon* CD, went to Kinko's, and photocopied the entire script. I still have that script, in the same three-ring notebook that stores my Star Pics *Twin Peaks* collector cards. It's a prized possession, despite the fact that some punk who watches *FWWM* for the first time can find the script *while* they illegally stream the movie. Today's *Twin Peaks* fans will never understand what those lean years were like. (Subtitled in The Red Room as "Hey, kid, turn down that music and get off my zigzag lawn.")

Twenty-odd years later, I got a copy of an even earlier draft of *FWWM*, dated July 3, 1991. By this time, I was immersed in the world of *Twin Peaks* and had a ton of connections. I didn't have to steal it to read it. This is the draft that was written before they came up with the Chet Desmond (Chris Isaak) character. Lynch and Engels wrote the July 3 version, which I will refer to as Script1, and submitted it to Kyle MacLachlan, and he passed. They had no choice but to create a new agent to investigate the Teresa Banks murder. They created agent Chet Desmond to take up the bulk of the Deer Meadow screen time. Engels said, "The original script had Cooper. When we couldn't convince [MacLachlan] to do it, we just went to Chris Isaak. David was working with Chris. He was over at David's house. I don't think Chris had acted much, but he was very

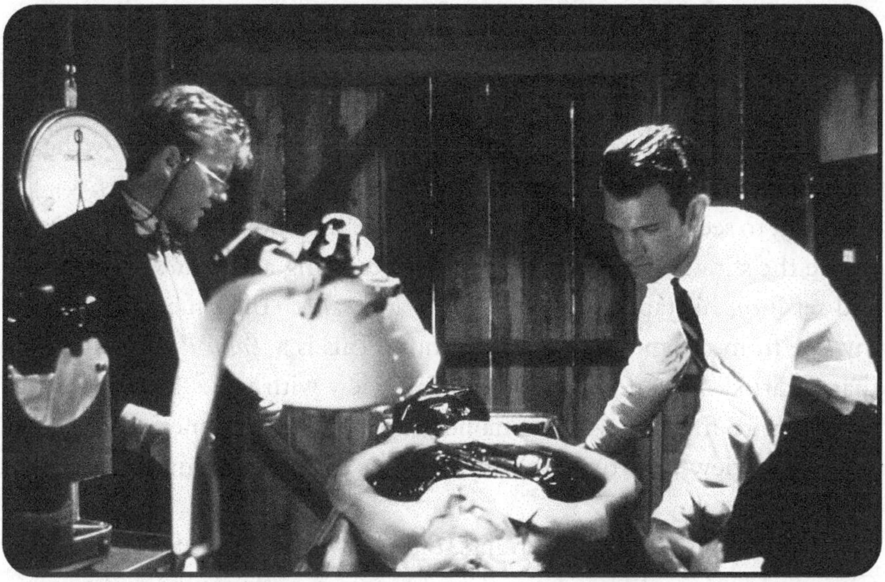

Kiefer Sutherland and Chris Isaak star in the first section of the film.
Photo courtesy of New Line Cinema

charming. The glory of the computer was that we just changed Cooper to Desmond in the script. We gave him an introduction, and we were prepared to do the entire sequel with just Chris. Then Kyle changed his mind and said he would do the film, but then we thought it was kind of cool to have two agents because we liked what we had, and MacLachlan would just do a few scenes."

I will refer to the script with Cooper and Desmond as Script2. This is the version I copied on that fateful day in the CD shop. In this chapter, I will compare and contrast those two scripts and then compare them with the final version of the film. If a scene is in all three or if the scene shows up in the *Missing Pieces*, I won't mention it here. This chapter points out only what changed during the writing process or what appeared in a script but was never seen by viewers (whether because it was never filmed or just edited out and lost, we don't know). My hope is that after this analysis, fans will start a kickstarter campaign for a "Missing Pieces of the *Missing Pieces*."

The first thing that shook me about the differences between Script1 and Script2 is there are no mentions of the Blue Rose in Script1. For me, as the managing editor of *The Blue Rose* magazine, this cut close to home. The Blue Rose has become a major mystery in the canon of *Twin Peaks*. Since Script1 doesn't have the disappearance of Chet Desmond, because he didn't exist, there really isn't any reason for the Blue Rose. So we have Chris Isaak to thank for the invention of the Blue Rose mysteries.

I went to see Chris Isaak in concert in 2019. I paid for a meet and greet before the show. When I met him, I was carrying a *Blue Rose* magazine, and set it on his table. He looked at it and said, "The Blue Rose! That's my line from the movie." I said, "I know. This is a *Twin Peaks* magazine that I started. I would like to do an interview with you." He said, "You do an entire magazine that is named after one of my lines? I'd love to do an interview with the guy who started a magazine from something I said."

He called his assistant over and told him to get my information. As Chris and I stepped away from the table to get a picture, he said to me, privately, "My people protect me from everything, but I really want to do this interview." I emailed his assistant many times—they never agreed to the interview. I have interviewed enough actors to know when they are being sincere with me. Chris Isaak wasn't even really talking to me when he said his people protect him. We took just a few steps from the table to the area where he took pictures with fans, but in those steps I entered his

I met Chris Isaak at one of his concerts and got this photo, but not an interview. Photo courtesy of Jennifer Ryan

bubble, and without an ounce of exaggeration, those were the loneliest steps I have ever taken in my life. I felt like I was standing next to Elvis Presley in the seventies. I just imagined this rock star going from town to town, having only a few seconds with fans but never really connecting. His people never gave me access to Chris Isaak. They said they kicked it upstairs and the request was declined. (Who is more upstairs than Chris Isaak? Shouldn't his excitement be enough?) My interview, just like Chet Desmond, vanished into thin air, but if this ever gets to you, Chris Isaak, just know I emailed your guy five times, and I am still ready for that interview.

DEER MEADOW

The film and both scripts start off with the murder of Teresa Banks and spend about thirty minutes on this topic. There are not that many differences between when the first act was carried by Agent Cooper versus Agent Desmond. In Script1, Cooper still struggles with the Deer Meadow Sheriff's Department. The lines in Script1 between Cooper and Sam Stanley (Kiefer Sutherland) are almost identical to those between Desmond and Sam in Script2. One line from the Deer Meadow segment that appears in Script1 but not in Script2, and I am sure was cut because it was especially Cooper-esque, is delivered when Deputy Cliff tells Cooper the coffee was fresh about two days ago: Cooper, after disabling Cliff with the same nose trick, tells the secretary, "There should always be a fresh cup of coffee in every law enforcement office."

In the film, Teresa lived at the Fat Trout Trailer Park. In Script1, it is called the Canyon Trailer Park. Also in Script1, Teresa's body washes up at Joseph's Creek, not Wind River, like in the film. Script1 specified that text would be overlaid on-screen indicating that it was 1988. It would have been great if that had made the final version just to cement the date, which we will discuss later on. Another small change is Hap's Diner, as it is known in the film, is referred to as Hap's Truck Stop.

In both scripts, but not in the film, the FBI agent—whether it is Cooper or Desmond—finds a Titleist golf ball under Teresa's trailer. This would be a connection to Leland Palmer, who plays golf, sometimes in his living room. (Hey, makes more sense than chopping wood in his living room. . . . *IN HIS LIVING ROOM*?)

PHILLIP JEFFRIES

In Script1, there is no disappearance of Chet, because there is no Chet. Cooper gives his "Who knows where or when?" speech, and then Lynch cuts to a year later and we head to Twin Peaks. In Script2, Chet disappears, Cooper tries to guess what is missing in Diane's office, Cole gets a call saying Chet has disappeared, and Cooper goes to investigate. The amazing thing is that neither script has Phillip Jeffries (David Bowie) appearing at this point, which is where the scene appears in the final film. Both scripts have Jeffries appearing in Cole's office in 1989 during the last seven days of Laura Palmer's life, not in 1988 during the Banks investigation.

In Script1 & Script2, we see Laura Palmer walking to school with Donna. Then we cut to the scene with Gordon, Cooper, Albert, and Jeffries in the FBI office. In the film version, the Jeffries scene takes place when Chet Desmond disappears, which makes it seem as if Desmond's disappearance leads to Jeffries's appearance, or that Jeffries's appearance is the reason Cooper is assigned to the case.

This, I theorized, had to be something Lynch decided in the editing process. I remembered that Albert gets a call and finds out that Desmond disappeared at the same time he calls the front desk to see if Jeffries ever even really arrived at the FBI building. How could Albert deliver the line that "Jeffries was never here" if the scene happened in 1989? Then I knew that the proof would depend on if we SEE Albert say Desmond disappeared or if we only HEAR him. If we actually see Miguel Ferrer's lips move while he says this line in *FWWM*, then I am wrong. If the camera is on someone else, then it could have been a voice-over that Lynch had Ferrer loop during editing. I checked the film, and sure enough, the camera is on Albert when he says, "I've got the front desk now. He was never here," but then it cuts to Gordon Cole when we *HEAR* Albert say, "And news from Deer Meadow: Agent Chester Desmond has disappeared." Think about it. That is one heck of a front desk that has all that information in one phone call. But with half the line in the shooting script, and half not, Lynch can link the appearance of Jeffries to the disappearance of Desmond, as they now occur at the same time.

A similar thing happens in the film at the end of this entire sequence: Cooper and Cole are checking the tape to see if Jeffries really did appear.

First we see Albert deliver the first two sentences. Then we see Cole when Albert mentions Desmond. Photos courtesy of New Line Cinema

The camera is in front of Cole, so we see his lips move when he says, "But where did he go?" However, when Cole says, "And where is Chester Desmond?" the point of view has switched, so we see Cole only from the back. The fact that both mentions of Desmond happen with looped-in voice-over proves that this was something Lynch decided on in editing—another clue that the film was still in flux in Lynch's mind while shooting.

This simple editing decision, having the Jeffries scene take place in 1988 instead of 1989, has huge ramifications for the mythology of *Twin Peaks* and causes David Lynch (and/or Mark Frost) to make a mistake in *The Return*, and possibly allows for an error in *FWWM*. In Script1 when Cole says, "May Day," Phillip Jeffries responds, "May? 1989?" In Script2, they caught the month mistake (Laura was murdered in February) and changed Jeffries's line to "February? 1989?" One could certainly question

Again the dialogue begins on the first shot, but Cole only mentions Desmond from behind, likely indicating that the lines were looped. Photos courtesy of New Line Cinema

why Cole saying "May Day" would cause Jeffries to wonder what month it is, but let's table that. Jeffries has had a really bad day. So while it was a good thing that they changed the line to February, it is really bad that they left Bowie saying 1989, because it isn't 1989 anymore; it is 1988, during the Teresa Banks investigation.

In the final version of *FWWM*, Jeffries just says "February," and they rightly cut the 1989 line, but in the *Missing Pieces* they let the 1989 line stand. Now, you could make a weak argument that maybe Jeffries heard in TRATCS that Laura Palmer would die in February 1989. (This makes no sense and is just me trying to throw Lynch a bone, because none of us are permitted to say he made a mistake or we lose our Bookhouse Boy badge.) I mean, the way the scene plays, Jeffries is obviously reacting to the fact that he has been gone for two years, so he should think it is 1987. Remember, the scripts have this scene placed in 1989. Cole yells, "You've been gone damn near two years." So Jeffries should have the realization that he time traveled. The scripts and the *Missing Pieces* have him in Buenos Aires and then traveling directly to Philadelphia. (Want to be more confused? Script1 has this scene taking place in Cole's Portland, Oregon, office rather than Philly; assuming this is because this scene was

The placement of this scene has ramifications in 2017.
Photo courtesy of New Line Cinema

supposed to be days before Laura dies and that is how Cooper got to Twin Peaks so quickly. The only reason we know they are in Philadelphia is because it is placed on the screen, another choice that could have been made in editing.)

Lynch decided in the editing phase, and brilliantly so, to place this scene in the year of Teresa Banks's murder. This is a better slot because it really would have been jumpy to go from Deer Meadow in 1988 to Twin Peaks in 1989, have Laura walk down the street for only a moment, then jump to the FBI for a quick Cooper scene, then jump to Buenos Aires, then back to the FBI, then to the Convenience Store meeting, and finally back to Laura picking up Donna for school. Can you imagine processing all that happens along with Jeffries's story and then popping back to the "Mike is the man" dialogue between Laura and Donna and keeping that straight in your mind? I can't keep this straight and I am writing it. My desk looks like a scene from *The Wire*, with scripts and screen captures spread all over the place.

No, this scene works better having happened after Chet disappears, so that we stay in the same year and change only locations. It introduces Cooper, Bob, MFAP, Cole, and Albert earlier in the film and brings a little bit of our familiar *Twin Peaks* cast to the front thirty minutes. Also, if this happened in 1988, it's more believable that Cooper doesn't discuss Jeffries with Cole or Albert when he sees them nine to fourteen days later in TOS. If he had materialized in 1988, they would have had time to discuss it before the events of 1989, and it wouldn't have been fresh on their minds when we first meet them in the series. Moving the scene to this section of the film is a much better decision, but it does cause a mistake in the long run, even if you excuse Jeffries from saying 1989, which I don't. But since Lynch did cut the 1989 line from the film, and we accept only the film (and not the *Missing Pieces*) as canon, what is the mistake?

The mistake presents itself twenty-five years later, in 2017, when *Twin Peaks* came back to television as *The Return* on Showtime. In Part 15, Bad Cooper goes to see Phillip Jeffries, who is now a steaming device in-between two worlds. (No, I will not explain why. But I hope someone who never saw *The Return* just read that line and threw this book in the trash can.) Bad Cooper says to Jeffries, "In 1989, you came to FBI headquarters and didn't want to talk about Judy." Lynch then cuts to this exact scene from *FWWM* with David Bowie saying, "We're not gonna talk about Judy." This is an error, because this should be 1988, not 1989. In the shooting script it was 1989, but as it played in the film, it was 1988, a year before Laura Palmer was killed. I am not sure how they made this mistake, because it is unlikely they went back to the shooting script to do research. But clearly it was 1988 when Jeffries appeared, which means he disappeared in 1986. If these last few paragraphs left you more confused than drinking a few Black Yukon Sucker Punches with Judge Sternwood, then just move on and forget it. But to my *Twin Peaks* scholars out there, pretty darn interesting, huh? I guess I have to turn in my Bookhouse badge now.

In Script2, the Phillip Jeffries scene in Cole's office happens in 1989. They wrote in the script that on the screen it says: *Exactly* seven days before the murder of Laura Palmer. But when Cooper walks into Cole's office, he says, "Gordon, it is 10:10 on February 15" (no year was specified). February 15 wouldn't be *exactly* seven days before her death. It would be eight days. Luckily, someone caught this error, and Cooper's line in the film was changed to February 16.

In both scripts, Jeffries mentions Judy, although in Script1 he just says, "I'm not gonna talk about her," and then refers to "her" as Judy in a later line. I don't want to live in a world where the line "I'm not gonna talk about Judy" doesn't exist. But who is Judy? Well, that argument could last a lifetime. While I will discuss *The Return* here and there in this book, for the most part I am focusing just on *FWWM*. The film was written immediately after TOS, which connects them pretty closely. (This can be seen by the addition of the Titleist golf ball. It's doubtful Lynch would remember that detail in 2012 when he started cowriting *The Return* with Mark Frost.) Lynch and Engels didn't have years to rethink the canon. Within the confines of *FWWM*, the idea behind Judy was that she was Josie's sister. Jeffries had some connection with her that led him to Buenos Aires.

Robert Engels told me for *The Blue Rose* #2, "Judy is my wife's sister's name, so that is where we got the name. My wife, Jill Engels, played Trudy, the waitress at the Great Northern, in the series. That is how I got the idea of using my wife's sister's name." When I asked him if Judy was

Josie's sister, he said, "Oh yeah, I think that is true. The doorknob thing was huge. Josie is in the doorknob. What a conversation! [Laughs.] There was a whole thing about who Judy was. There was a relationship. Judy was somehow related with Agent Cooper that we never got to."

In Script1, Phillip Jeffries tells Cole, "[Judy's] sister's there, too. [a little doubtful] At least part of her." Josie's head is stuck in a doorknob, according to Episode 23 of TOS, so it is feasible that only "part of her" (i.e., her head) could be in TRATCS. In all fairness, Script1 does NOT ever mention the Convenience Store meeting; it is only implied. Script2 adds that Jeffries had "been to one of their meetings." As far as proof that Lynch believed Josie's head was stuck in between two worlds, we know from Richard Beymer's behind-the-scenes photos of the filming of Episode 29, directed by Lynch in 1991, that Lynch was working on having a body double play Josie's head poking through the curtains in The Red Room. As the story goes, Joan Chen was not available, so this scene was cut. (See photo below, courtesy of Richard Beymer.)

Now you might just say, "Hey, Scott, Josie got stuck in the doorknob later in the timeline of *Twin Peaks*, and this Jeffries scene takes place way before Josie 'died.' So you are wrong and we want to ban you from the Twin Peaks Festival." Well, you have to remember that time does not matter in The Red Room. There actually is a line toward the end

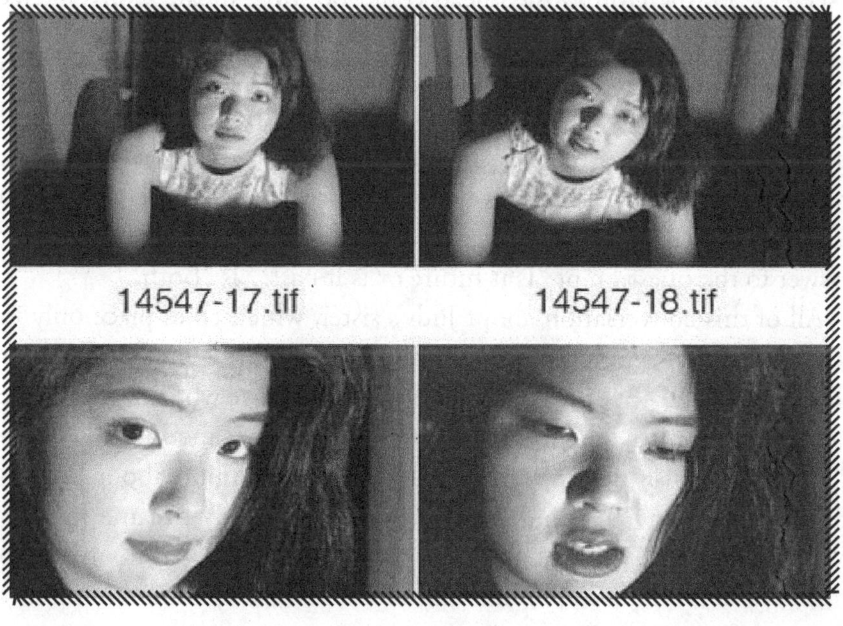

Josie got stuck in a doorknob in the series. How did that affect a line of dialogue in the script? Photo courtesy of CBS

of Script2 where MFAP says, "The later events have never been kept a secret." So, therefore, Josie's head could be stuck in the Convenience Store/Waiting Room/Red Room before *and* after she wound up in the doorknob. This also would explain why Cooper appears in The Red Room in Laura's dream in *FWWM before* he is trapped there, as well as why Jeffries knows there is something wrong with Cooper when he meets him in Cole's office. His first words regarding Cooper are "Who do you think that is there?" There is plenty of evidence that the correct answer to the question of "Is it future or is it past?" is "Both."

All of this conversation about Judy's sister, which takes place only in Script1, happens without Cooper present. I am sure Lynch and Engels did this so that Cooper wouldn't have this knowledge when he began the Palmer case. This is not to say that the Judy who is mentioned in *The Return* is Josie's sister. I believe Lynch changed his mind about Judy in the time between 1991 and 2012, which is why Judy became Jowday. (Which personally was a plot point I never liked. There was no reason to change the pronunciation, but that is just my personal opinion.) As to whether Judy becomes a spirit that inhabits Sarah Palmer in *The Return*, I don't know. This is all just to say where the idea of Judy began. Tracing the path from Script1 to Script2 to *FWWM* to *The Return* is a fun way to watch a mystery build, change, and grow in the mind of David Lynch with the help of collaborators Mark Frost and Robert Engels.

As we leave the Deer Meadow/Phillip Jeffries part of the scripts, it is interesting to note that the Twin Peaks/Laura Palmer section becomes the main focus on page thirty-five in Script1 and page forty-one in Script2. That means there is only a six-page differential between the two, but those six pages make all the difference in the world, and my world especially. Those six pages brought to the world the Blue Rose, Judy, TRATCS, the Formica table, Chet Desmond, and the Woodsman. Sounds to me like six is the number of completion.

LAURA, DONNA, AND THE MAN

I always thought it was genius that in the filmed version of *FWWM*, Laura, outside of the Hayward house, calls out, "Donna," and then Moira Kelly walks out. I figured this was done to let audiences know that Moira Kelly would now play Donna. But upon reading both scripts, I discovered that both always had Laura calling out to Donna. Lara Flynn Boyle passed on reprising her role as Donna Hayward to star in *Wayne's World*. I leave it up to you to decide if that was a better career choice. *Wayne's World* went on to gross over $120 Million, and *FWWM* grossed under $10 million, but I am pretty certain no one is writing essays in 2022 about the hidden meaning of the gun rack her character made for Wayne. Schwing!

There is dialogue in both scripts between Donna and Laura about schoolwork that Donna is helping Laura with. This scene outside the house was changed during filming so that Bobby and Mike offer to give them a ride to school and the line "Mike is the man" is added. Remember, in Script2 it is directly after Laura walks to pick up Donna that we were supposed to see the Phillip Jeffries Buenos Aires scene. That ends with the hotel bellhop screaming "Are you the man?" when Phillip reappears on the staircase. Then we would come back to Mike and Bobby saying "Mike is the man." This line is not in the script and might have been something Lynch added on set because he knew that the bellhop said the line about "the man" in the scene before, but the bellhop got cut. The scripted versions do not have the bellhop saying "Are you the man?" They also don't have Bobby, Mike, Donna, and Laura saying "Mike is the man." The scripts refer to MFAP as Mike. So it isn't too far of a leap to say that Lynch wanted to connect these events. Mike is also the name of the alter ego of the OAM, who is connected to MFAP. To make matters more confusing, MFAP is played by Michael J. Anderson, and Lynch refers to him as "Little Mike." So keep all those "Mikes" and "Mans" as straight as you can.

In both scripts, Mike Nelson meets Donna at school rather than on the way to school and tells her she needs a "real man." Donna responds, "Are you the real man?" That line might have sparked Lynch to improvise the "Mike is the man" scene outside the Hayward house while filming. Laura sees James before she pops into the bathroom to do a line of coke. In the film, we see them interact, but in the scripts they plan their rendezvous in the gym (see below).

James Marshall, Sheryl Lee, and Moira Kelly in a scene that is seen but not heard in the film. Photo courtesy of New Line Cinema

SMILES, THE HAYWARDS, AND HAROLD

While Script1 doesn't have the scene with Bobby, Laura, and Donna fighting outside the school, Script2 does have Bobby confronting Laura about where she was when he was looking for her. In one of the most classic scenes in the film, Laura calms Bobby down by making him smile. I just can't imagine this scene not existing. This scene, more than any other, visually displays the power that Laura Palmer possesses. Viewers are told over and over in TOS that Laura was loved by everyone, but they also know she was a difficult person. This scene shows how she used her charms to get what she wanted. It also is a great example for future filmmakers and writers of how to *show* an audience something instead of *telling* the audience something. Laura (and Sheryl Lee) harnesses this smile to capture Bobby (and the audience) and make everyone forget that she was just in a scene cheating on her boyfriend with James. Script2 includes a line for Sheryl Lee to say: "Oh come on, sweetie, give me one of your smiles." Thankfully, Lynch cut this and let Sheryl Lee act this moment. We do not need dialogue to figure out what she is doing; she just has to smile that smile, and the world will smile right back. It is a power that Laura utilizes to get drugs and to hide her most awful secrets. This film is full of dramatic moments that display the amazing talents of Sheryl Lee. Here is one that empowers the warmth, charisma, and almost

Laura Palmer smiles and "everybody run." Photo courtesy of New Line Cinema

superhuman charm that Sheryl Lee possesses as a person. In real life, she has smiled this smile at me. We are all fortunate that she didn't ask me to try to score some coke off a longhaired, wife-beating drug dealer, because I'd happily be writing this book from prison right now.

After school, inside the Hayward house, Donna's mother, Eileen, checks to see if the girls have enough nuts to snack on. This is a scene that is not in the *Missing Pieces*, but there is a photo of it. So one assumes it was either filmed and lost or that Lynch chose not to include it in the *Missing Pieces*. We know there are other scenes that weren't released. Robert Engels told me, "There was a lot more shot that wasn't used in the *Missing Pieces*. I do know we shot a scene with fire, because the actor in that scene was a classmate of mine in theater school. He was in town and was perfect for it. I know that we shot that because I came by to see him. It was on a stairway and he was talking about Judy, and the stairway caught on fire." That scene will be used in 2024's CBS box set called *No, This Time We Really Mean It: The Super Duper Complete Mystery*.

A quick aside on the *Missing Pieces*: did you know that it never says *Missing Pieces* in the credits for that film? It just says, "What you are about to see are missing pieces," and then in the end credits it says *Twin Peaks: Fire Walk With Me Deleted Scenes*. Another example of how names in the *Twin Peaks* world are never without debate or confusion. Do we call it the *Missing Pieces* or not? Do we call it Season 3 or *The Return*? Do we use the episode titles or episode numbers? Nothing can be easy for this fandom. (Of course you don't use the episode titles. Any civilized human knows that.)

Back at the Hayward house: Script1 does not have the "falling in space dialogue," but Script2 does. Neither has the line "And the angels wouldn't help you, because they are all gone." The Angel does not appear in *any* of the scripts at all, and seems to be something Lynch added as a through line on set. Sheryl Lee has said The Angel was key for her. It might have been developed on set to bring Lee back to herself. Sheryl Lee told me in *The Blue Rose* #8, "What was so important about walking away from that character originally was that she got an angel. For me, that was the hope."

The scripts generally follow the film through the Harold Smith scene, though one difference is that Laura says the entire *FWWM* poem to

Lenny Von Dohlen plays shut-in Harold Smith. His character spawned a Facebook Live event during the COVID quarantine.
Photo courtesy of New Line Cinema

Harold: "Thru the darkness of future past, the magician longs to see, one chants out between two worlds, 'Fire walk with me.'" As an aside, there used to be a ton of online discussion about whether it was "one chance out" or "one chants out." It is written in the script as chants. I also asked Al Strobel when I interviewed him for *The Blue Rose* #13. He said, "Chants. It is kind of hard to pronounce. It was also written on a piece of paper." So that puts that mystery to rest.

In Script1, Laura asks Harold if he is Bob and says that if so, he should kill her now. He suggests she confide in James about what she is going through, but she says, "James is in love with a dead girl." James may have always been cool, but I think Bob was a little out of his wheelhouse.

MEALS ON WHEELS

In the scripts and the film, the story goes back to the FBI office, where Albert and Cooper discuss the word association game that Cole had them do when Jeffries appeared. All of this is cut from the film, because once Lynch moved this scene back to 1988, they wouldn't be discussing a word association game about something that happened a year earlier. I have always wondered why the edit to Albert and Cooper talking was so strange. It fades in and you can see Kyle MacLachlan's lips moving, but you can't hear his dialogue. (The line you can't hear is "The name and memory of Teresa Banks is haunting me.") Lynch faded in to the middle of Cooper's line, where he says, "Lately, I have been filled with the knowingness [in the filmed version, he thankfully says "knowledge"] that the murderer will strike again." This is more proof that when filming took place, the expectation was that the Phillip Jeffries scenes would occur during the Laura Palmer section of the film.

The only difference in the Double R scene in which Laura prepares for her Meals on Wheels runs is that Script2 has Big Ed and Nadine entering the diner and Nadine wanting to leave when she sees Norma. This is shown in the *Missing Pieces*, but was not in Script1. Strangely, in Script1 Norma still cries when Laura and Shelly leave; this scene makes no sense without Big Ed coming in with Nadine. In the *Missing Pieces*, Big Ed comes back to say they will meet up; this wasn't in either script.

Both scripts have Laura returning home with Mrs. Tremond's picture for her wall and then seeing Leland coming out of the house. Both scripts also include a scene in which a woman comes upon Laura as she cries while hiding under the bush. To cover up the truth, Laura pretends she lost her half-heart necklace and then claims to have found it. Following this scene, Laura goes back into the house and looks around to see if Bob is still under the fan. There is no Bob. This is Laura trying to piece together whether Leland is Bob or not. Another bit of naming controversy in the *Twin Peaks* world is the spelling of Bob's name. The scripts spell his name Bob, not BOB.

In the *Missing Pieces*, Laura then runs to the Hayward house. The scene in the *Missing Pieces* has Doc Hayward telling Laura, "The angels will return, and when you see the one that is meant to help you, you will weep with joy." This line of dialogue is not in the script (remember, there are no mentions of angels anywhere in the script). This scene is such a great example of the way David Lynch's mind works. This dialogue is a setup for the end of the movie, where Laura sees her angel and weeps with joy. Lynch cuts it, but leaves the ending intact. As a filmmaker, he doesn't mind *cutting* the gun out of Act 1 *and* allowing it to show up in Act 4. So take that, Chekhov!

In Script1 only, after Laura leaves, Donna asks Doc if he thinks Laura is troubled. Donna thinks something is different about her. While it would always be great to see more scenes with Warren Frost, this is a good cut, as it is better if it is not thrown in our face how much Donna sees of Laura's troubles in *FWWM* without mentioning them in TOS.

LAURA'S PICTURE

That night we have Laura's dream, which includes some significant changes among the scripts and final version. One interesting detail is that both scripts describe the location for Laura's dream as "In Mrs. Tremond's Picture." They do not specify the room with the wallpaper is located in the Black Lodge or The Red Room. So while this wallpaper and these doors will be shown again in *The Return*, when Bad Cooper walks past them after entering through the Convenience Store, there wasn't any explicit connection specified in the script of *FWWM*. Remember, these are scripts fans were never supposed to see, so there would have been no reason for Lynch to refrain from calling the location exactly what he thought it was, and clearly he thought of it as simply "In Mrs. Tremond's Picture." He had no reason to assume that some day a fool like me would be studying it like it was the Torah.

As the camera glides from room to room, both scripts describe Mrs. Tremond's grandson holding his hands above him as if he were grasping an imaginary glass ball. One wonders if it could have even been a golden orb? Then a ring of fire appears, and the camera moves through that and into The Red Room. This is the same ring of fire that Bob and MFAP go through in Jeffries's description of the meeting he attended (see the Ron Garcia interview in Chapter 7 for an amazing connection to this). One imagines the ring of fire became too expensive to create back in 1992, because that type of special effects was expensive. It's interesting that in *FWWM*, this hallway and door maze are an entrance to The Red Room, but in *The Return* this entrance brings Bad Cooper to Phillip Jeffries as the steam-creating device. This jives with Episode 29 of TOS, in which Cooper appears to be going down the same hallway multiple times but always ends up somewhere else. The path may look the same, but the destination seems to depend on who is making the trek. (I could think about that one sentence all day.)

In Script1, when Laura's arm goes dead during her dream and she

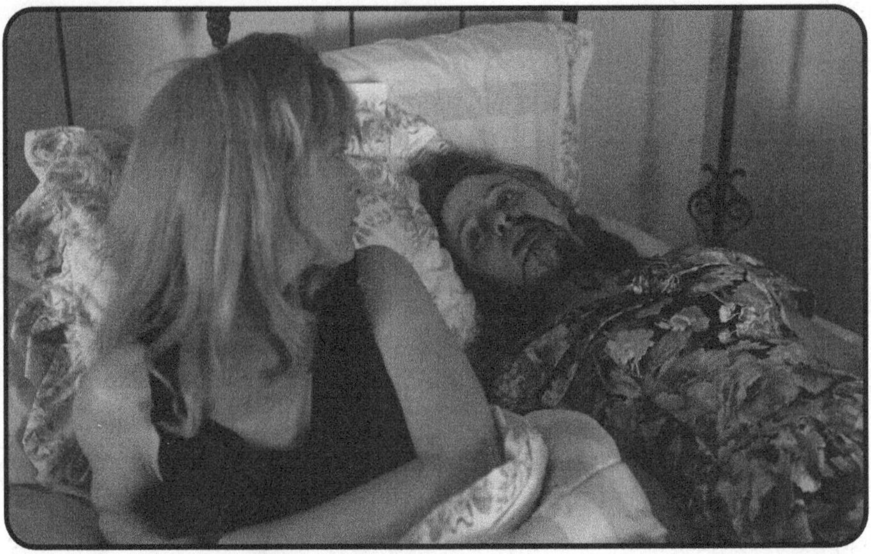

Let us be thankful that it was Annie Blackburn (Heather Graham) in bed with Laura and not Lynch's first choice. Photo courtesy of New Line Cinema

looks at the door and back to the bed, it is Cooper who is in bed with her. In Script2 and the film, it is Annie Blackburn (Heather Graham). Remember that when Lynch and Engels wrote Script1, they had no idea Kyle MacLachlan was going to turn them down, so there was no reason to not use Cooper whenever and however they wanted. When they had to limit his role, Lynch decided to replace him with Annie Blackburn. In the rest of the Cooper scenes, he was replaced by Chet Desmond. A really interesting thought would be what if they had Chet Desmond in bed with Laura? That idea will keep me up for hours tonight wondering how that would have changed the mythology. What if Agent Chet Desmond and Laura Palmer had interacted? What would it mean for where Chet had gone?

But back to when Lynch was under the impression MacLachlan would be in the film as much as he needed him to be. Lynch wrote in Script1 that Laura asks Cooper, "Why didn't you help me sooner?" Cooper pulls her to him, kisses her, and starts to make love to her. We hear Sarah call out Laura's name. Then Cooper disappears. Let's thank the Fireman that this scene was never filmed. Had Cooper and Laura started to make love, it would have put Cooper in the same category as every other man who tried to take sexual advantage of this poor high school girl. While I completely understand that this was Laura's dream, it sure would have undercut MacLachlan's contention that he had refused to proceed with the Season 2 storyline of Cooper and Audrey getting together because he thought it was inappropriate for an FBI agent to date a high schooler.

Let's just be thankful that it is Heather Graham as Annie in bed with Laura and that she delivers the line "Write it in your diary." Not just because it became the inspiration for the title of this very chapter, but also because it played a major part in *The Return*, and gave Lynch something to think about for twenty-five years. David Lynch said in *Lynch on Lynch*, "I've got to say the one thing about that scene—where Annie suddenly appears in Laura's bed. This is before Laura has been murdered, and before Coop has come in Twin Peaks. Annie appears, filled with blood, and wearing the exact same dress that she's wearing when she was in The Red Room with Cooper in the series—in the future. She says to Laura, 'The good Dale is in the Lodge and he can't leave. Write it in your diary.' And I know that Laura wrote that down, in a little side space in her diary. Now if *Twin Peaks*, the series, had continued, someone may've found that. It's like someone in 1920 saying 'Lee Harvey Oswald' or something, and then later you sort of see it all. I had hopes of something coming out of that, and I liked the idea of the story going back and forth in time." Annie's line and her appearance in that scene were obviously a very important addition for Lynch, and something he never forgot.

The rest of the dream is the same. The description of the dream's end in both scripts mentions Laura standing in the picture looking down at herself sleeping in bed. This is technically what we see in the film, but I never considered that Laura was actually looking down at herself sleeping. I could see her in the picture, and I always liked this moment because Laura becomes framed in the picture swaying back and forth with a look on her face of such ambivalence. We as viewers are watching her in an actual moving picture. Isn't that how we met Laura to begin with? We watched her on our television screen, which is basically a framed moving picture. Laura Palmer became very famous for being in a framed picture, not just on television but also in her homecoming photograph. She is known for hanging on walls and being framed. I viewed this as a meta moment in the film. Laura is trapped in her own dream, in which she has

Laura in a picture in a frame watching herself as we watch her through a framed screen. Photo courtesy of New Line Cinema

to die so that the audience can be introduced to the town of Twin Peaks. She is literally becoming a piece of art. So much so that she becomes a part of a framed painting hanging on a wall for us to look at. So when Lynch cuts to her sleeping in bed, I always assumed that was to show us that she was in bed dreaming. She woke up and the ring was not in her hand. But according to the scripts, Laura is in the picture looking at herself asleep. I have to admit that until I read the scripts for this book, I never thought Laura was looking at herself sleeping. Did you?

PARTYLAND

James drives by the Palmer house on his motorcycle and talks to Laura as Leland watches. This scripted scene does take place in the film but later. The scene has a bit more dialogue and is followed by the *Missing Pieces* scene in which Laura leans alongside the wall of the stairs under the fan in the Palmer house. Bob has scripted dialogue ("I am glad you let me talk to you. You used to not let me talk to you.") as Laura stands there. This is not in the film or in the *Missing Pieces*. Maybe if Frank Silva had been alive in 2014, when the *Missing Pieces* was released, Lynch would have had him come in and do the voice-over. Most likely, this scene was cut before the final edit back in 1992, or the voice-over might have been lost over the years. Either way, there is no voice-over. This is followed by the *Missing Pieces* scene with Laura, Sarah, and her sweater.

Donna, Laura, Buck, and Tommy all drive from The Roadhouse to a bar in Canada, a scene that is shown in the *Missing Pieces.* One change from script to screen is that in the scripts Buck does a war whoop in Laura's face on the drive to the bar, and there is a flashback to MFAP making this sound in her dream. Also, in the scripts Donna makes out with Buck in the car. I am forever grateful that I didn't have to watch sweet Donna Hayward make out with BUCK. In Script1, Donna snorts cocaine after being pressured by Laura. In Script2, she refuses and says she doesn't need to take this to be Laura's friend. Laura calls her a downer, as she does in the *Missing Pieces.*

They enter the bar, which is not called in either script The Power and the Glory, as it is in the *Missing Pieces* scene where we see them enter the bar from the outside. It is listed in the script as Partyland. Although if you go by the end credits to the film, the band in this bar is the Power and the Glory, so who knows what the name of this bar is? (Hmm, not another naming issue?) Also, the dialogue here does not indicate subtitling in the scripts, as it does in the Red Room and TRATCS scenes. (There will be more on the subtitles and the overall Partyland scene in Chapter 9.)

In Script1, Jacques Renault puts a red pill on Donna's tongue and then holds her head in his hands as he tells her there is no tomorrow. So in Script1, Donna takes a lot of drugs. In Script2, Donna takes no drugs at all. In the film version, Buck tricks her by putting a pill in her beer and Laura says, "Chug-a-lug Donna." That line is not in either script. But don't you worry: Jacques's "I am as blank as a fart" is in all versions, as it should be.

In both scripts men mount Laura and Ronette from behind, and the two girls end up face-to-face as they say, "Here we go again." In the film, Laura points to Buck to service her under the table, which gives her more power and control over the situation and is much more effective than the scripted version of having someone mount her from behind. But the booth scene that appears in the film was not scripted.

In the scripts, when Laura sees Donna topless making out with

Tommy, Bob's voice says to her, "See what we can do to Donna." This line is not in the film, even though the scene is. If you look at Sheryl Lee's face, it is easy to imagine this is what she is hearing. It's amazing how many times Bob had voice-over lines in the scripts that didn't make it into the film. These lines jived extremely well with *The Secret Diary of Laura Palmer* by Jennifer Lynch, which had Bob talking with Laura quite a bit. The only voice-over by Frank Silva as Bob that made it into the final edit of *FWWM* is when he says, "I want to taste through your mouth" as Laura stands under the fan, which is used to cover up the previously discussed fade-in line as Cooper and Albert talk about the word association game. Why Lynch wanted this one Bob voice-over to happen is unknown, although I always felt the less we saw or heard from Bob the scarier he was. It probably wouldn't have been my choice to have him as a bouncing Silly Putty ball in *The Return*, but no one asked me.

A BIT OF TWIN PEAKS AND THE LAST DAY

Back to the scripts: the next morning, there's a scene with Nadine skinning a deer for Big Ed, a pointless scene with Pete and Catherine trading uninteresting insults, and a scene with Truman and Josie talking about going public with their relationship as Truman gently strums a guitar and talks about not wanting to eat fish eyeballs. This trilogy of scenes, all cut from the film, would have made it seem more like an episode of *Twin Peaks*, cutting around town and moving away from the Laura Palmer story. Cutting these scenes was the correct decision. Not just because they are pointless in any context, but also because they really would have slowed the film down and taken the gas off the destructive ride that Laura Palmer is on. They also skew more closely to the rocky part of Season 2. An interesting comparison, seeing how Lynch is thought of as not ever having anything to do with the lackluster Season 2 section of *Twin Peaks*.

Tuesday, two days before the murder, Leland says during breakfast with Laura and Sarah that it is Johnny Horne's birthday. Leland, Johnny, Jerry Horne, Sylvia Horne, and Ben Horne all celebrate Johnny's birthday in Ben's office. Sylvia confronts Ben as to why he has a picture of Laura but not Audrey in his office. After the *Missing Pieces* scene of Harry, Andy, and Hawk in the sheriff's station, Laura pops in to see Ben and kisses him when he gives her a packet of coke. While some of the scenes that are outside of the Laura story should have been cut, it might have been interesting to see Laura interact with Johnny and Ben Horne. But then again, it would have been late into the film to start adding in all these characters from the series. All these cuts show superb discipline in filmmaking.

In Script2 only, before Bobby and Laura head to the woods to meet up with Deputy Cliff from Deer Meadow, Pete stops at Big Ed's Gas Farm to fill up. Big Ed and Pete discuss being on empty, and Ed cleans Pete's windshield inside and out. They talk about being glad they are not with their wives.

After Bobby kills Deputy Cliff, there is in both scripts another scene with Laura in the stairwell under the fan, as Bob says he wants her to kill for him. She says, "You'll have to kill me." It is unlikely that this is from the same *Missing Pieces* scene in which she smiles because of the outfit she wears. More likely, the smile scene is from when Sarah asks about the sweater. This "kill for me" scene was either never filmed or lost.

We come to the final night of Laura's life: neither script has Laura seeing someone behind James when they are in the woods and she screams. This becomes an important plot point in *The Return*. Another interesting moment in both scripts is that when Laura leaves James at Sparkwood and 21, the camera is instructed to pan off to the side of the road to find the wilted red rose from Doc Hayward's magic trick shown in the *Missing Pieces*. How interesting if the film had had both a red rose and a blue rose. Maybe I could have started two magazines?

At Jacques's cabin, we see Laura with the poker chip in her mouth. In Script1, Jacques says, "Bite the bullet, baby." In Script2, Leo says, "Bite the bullet, baby." One wonders if they watched Episode 7 to make sure they had the correct person saying the line. According to what Jacques tells Cooper in Episode 7 (notice I use the episode number and not the title, because I am not an animal), it was Leo who put the chip in her mouth and said it. Didn't matter, because this part wasn't shown in *FWWM* or the *Missing Pieces*.

Outside the train car, OAM has a line of dialogue in both scripts. He says, "That's his own daughter you're killing." He laughs and runs away. Another piece of the puzzle to decipher as to where OAM's loyalty lies. I asked Al Strobel if he thought OAM was a good or bad guy. He said, "All of it. How I arrived at that is that my character was of the very few that was allowed to change throughout the whole thing. First I was the red herring. Then I kind of became an ally for Cooper to use to understand things more. Then some negative, evil stuff snuck in there. I got to be a scary character and then I evolved to The Red Room *maître d'*."

Leland enters The Red Room after killing Laura, and Gerard and MFAP say in unison, "Bob, you are not going home without me." Then Gerard and MFAP deliver the garmonbozia line. In both scripts, when Leland floats up in the air, he splits into two: one is Leland and one is Bob (half faded). Only Script2 mentions that Leland has a wound. When asked by A.M. Starr from 1400 River Road, a *Twin Peaks*-themed blog, if the blood on his shirt was Laura's blood or a wound, Ray Wise said, "It was a wound, and it was self-inflicted. I never told anyone that. It was guilt that made me do that. Sort of like a hara-kiri suicide. I didn't kill myself, but I wounded myself."

This is where Script1 ends. Script2 goes on to include the Annie/Cooper ending that is shown in the *Missing Pieces*. Then it says that Laura sits on Cooper's lap in The Red Room. Again, let us be thankful that they didn't stage the scene that way; it's remarkably better that Cooper never sexualized Laura Palmer. It does not reference the all-important Angel that appears to have brought joy to Laura and Sheryl Lee. It does not mention her smiling, laughing, or crying. The filmed version certainly has a much happier feel. Reading the ending to both scripts just doesn't do justice to the acting, directing, and music all colliding together to become the end of this film. But I suppose that is the difference between scriptwriting and moviemaking.

CHAPTER 6

Let's Rock

The most meta moment in all of *Twin Peaks* has to be the line from Episode 2 "There is always music in the air." The original series pretty much had wall-to-wall music at a time when television scoring were less sophisticated than movies. The impact that composer and arranger Angelo Badalamenti had on television is never appropriately acknowledged. I recently did a rewatch of *China Beach*, which premiered two years before *Twin Peaks* but also ended in 1991. The first two seasons use the same musical refrain for every dramatic scene. In the final two seasons, the episodes were scored with scene-specific music. I have no proof that there is cause and effect, but you know what happened between Season 2 and 3 of *China Beach*? *Twin Peaks* premiered. The difference between shows in the eighties and shows in the nineties is striking when it comes to scores. The television soundtrack was growing up right before our eyes at that time. Angelo Badalamenti brought a sophisticated jazz score to the small screen, which just wasn't being done at that time.

He continued his complex work in *FWWM*. The musical score is so omnipresent in the film that it sometimes rivals the dialogue as the primary sound. In the Pink Room scene, it literally overtakes the dialogue, and subtitles had to be added to understand what the characters were saying because the music was louder than the actors' words. On top of the amazing score, Lynch adds war whoops, ominous whooshes, and plenty of wind blowing. There is nary a moment in the film without some sort of music playing. At the end of this chapter, I compile a complete list of the forty-nine unique songs that are used in the film (double-checked and approved by Ross Dudle of the *Twin Peaks* Soundtrack Design website). The list does not count repeat playings. All the songs but one are written by either Badalamenti and/or Lynch. That is a lot of music to keep track of. Those of you who think my claim that Sheryl Lee gives the best performance ever is just fan-based hyperbole will love this statement even more: Badalamenti composed the best score of all time for *FWWM*. (Take that John Williams, you Oscar-nominated slacker!)

I often wonder what Badalamenti thought when David Lynch told him that there would be a full movie to score only one year after the series ended. Badalamenti had just enjoyed the biggest success of his career with his album of music from the television series, peaking at number twenty-two on the Billboard charts, achieving gold status, and even winning a Grammy. Now he had to come up with a completely new *Twin Peaks* score. Should he use the same songs or write new ones? Would those new tracks meet the bar set by the original songs? He didn't cower from the task; as always, he rose to the occasion, and created his best composition ever when he wrote . . .

"THEME FROM TWIN PEAKS: FIRE WALK WITH ME"

(For extra fun, listen to the songs that correlate with their section.) Badalamenti begins the theme with a throbbing synth sound that evokes fear, anxiety, and the pulse of a spinning ceiling fan. All this in only the first thirty seconds of music. A muted trumpet comes in, playing a hauntingly sexy melody. Later, at about 3:45 into the song, a wandering bass enters the orchestration to bring some jazz/rock feel to it. So we have sex from the trumpet, fear from the synth, and rock 'n' roll from the plucking bass. What do you get when you mix sex, fear, and rock 'n' roll together? You get Laura Palmer, the star of the movie. The theme sets the tone for the entire film. The fact that he was brave enough to start the

All the MP3 cover art designs used in this chapter were created by Ross Dudle from twinpeakssoundtrackdesign.blogspot.com.

film with a new composition should have prepared audiences for what they were going to watch: SOMETHING NEW. Given the popularity of the television score at that time, Badalamenti could have taken the easy way out and just used "Laura Palmer's Theme," and viewers would have been fine. But he would have been dead wrong to use that song.

"Laura Palmer's Theme" played throughout the television series whenever a character mentioned or thought about Laura. The song is a melodramatic piece of music designed to evoke sadness and express mourning, with sweeping piano chords rising out of the dark synth sounds from the key of A flat and resolving into the friendly key of C. The theme starts at the low end of the keyboard and explodes with high piano notes that make us long to see Laura alive once again. It telegraphs perfectly what Sarah Palmer and the townsfolk of Twin Peaks are feeling. These are the people who miss their homecoming queen and the girl who prepared their Meals on Wheels. What it doesn't do is represent the living Laura Palmer. The Laura we meet in *FWWM* could not be scored with rolling piano arpeggios. Badalamenti knew what his feature-film task was—to let us know that we would be meeting not the postmortem version of Laura that the town created to soothe their guilt, but a Laura who was very much alive, tangled up in sex, depression, and the fight against good and evil. The new composition captures these qualities of the lead character in a way that few film themes ever have been able to. When all three parts of this composition collide, you can't help but feel exactly as Lynch wants you to: torn, scared, and wildly unsettled. That is the main goal of a musician who is hired to complement the filmmaker with music. "Laura Palmer's Theme" is who Laura's friends and family wanted her to be. "Theme From Twin Peaks Fire Walk With Me" is who she actually was.

> "We started getting into this cool jazz thing and a lot of weird bowing on the bass. The opening title was just a rhythm section of piano, bass, and drums. It was the only time I used a muted trumpet, and then in the middle it became very dark, but it still felt cool. Melodically, I am planting the seed that it's gonna be cool, but watch out!"
>
> - Angelo Badalamenti, Criterion Blu-ray bonus feature

"THE PINK ROOM"/"BLUE FRANK"

While the main score is written by Angelo Badalamenti, David Lynch contributed a few tracks to the film. The two Lynch tracks that I want to focus on play in the Pink Room scene. This is the bar in Canada where Laura, Donna, Jacques, Buck, and Tommy go for a simple night on the town. The scene is an assault on our senses from the get-go. The room is bathed in red light, making it hard to see, and the music is turned up so loud that the characters cannot be heard. It's like trying to have dinner at a hip bar where the manager thinks the patrons are there to hear the Muzak and not our own scintillating conversation. When I guested on *Twin Peaks Unwrapped* podcast #140 with host Bryon Kozaczka to talk about the music from the film, I mentioned something that I thought everyone was aware of. After the appearance, Twitter informed me that many people didn't know that two different songs played during this scene. The scene lasts for nine minutes. It starts with a blast of guitar that begins "The Pink Room" song. Upon reflection, I think this scene is not unlike Part 8 of *The Return*, where Lynch uses "Threnody to the Victims of Hiroshima" to assault viewers into aural submission while

visually immersing them in the inner workings of a hydrogen bomb exploding for an equal length of nine minutes of screen time. The Pink Room scene is certainly topped by Part 8 when it comes to aural assault, but it now seems like a stepping-stone in Lynch's sound development as a filmmaker. In The Pink Room, it is done with dark red lights and hypnotic guitar riffs by the band The Power and the Glory (played by the band Fox Bat Strategy). Lynch loves to lull viewers into a mood using lighting and music.

David Lynch talked about writing "The Pink Room" in a YouTube video called "David Lynch Fox Bat Strategy Behind The Music." He said, "I was standing in the hallway, and I heard this bass thing in my head. So I wrote down the kind of thing that would remind me of the steps. I went up to Don Falzone and said, 'This is the bass line.' And I hummed it to him. He started to play it. Then Steve [Hodges] started to go on the drums and then Andy [Armer] started going, and it got this thing going. They laid down this long track of this thing. Then Dave Jaurequi showed up. I said, 'This is kind of a fifties thing.' And he floated these chords over this thing."

The song "The Pink Room" plays for the first 4:30 of the scene. This is a guitar-and-drum-based song. Almost has the feel of a dance remix track without the uptempo computer beats. But it is the same few notes over and over again. During this part of the scene, the group is getting drunk and drugging Donna. Laura strips off her top and dances in the middle of the club. As the drugs kick in for Donna, the room spins, and a singular blue light bulb is shown as Ronette Pulaski appears. This is when the track changes to the song "Blue Frank." This is also written by Lynch. This track plays as the drugs have settled in. Laura does not feel anything anymore. Donna is shit-faced, and strips as well. This track has more of a Hindu bliss to it. It's impossible to hear it and not sway with the groove like you are Rick Rubin at a pot dispensary. This is no longer an assault on our ears. The change in the music is also reflected in the lighting of the scene. The red light is still prominent (this is The Pink Room, after all), but solid white flashes from the strobes light the characters' faces. Laura and Ronette are well lit, with an almost blue haze in the white strobes, as they sit in the booth and are serviced by Buck. The two songs, which many fans believed were just one, display the yin and the yang of a drunken night out, the consumption of the drug, and then the experience as the drug takes hold. The frankness of the earlier actions is completely on display as the scene ends to the sounds of "Blue Frank."

"BIRDS IN HELL"

The song sets up Laura Palmer's last day on Earth. This piece of music does its job spectacularly. There are only a few moments of complete silence in the film. But when Laura confronts her father and says, "Stay away from me," there is no music. There are no sound effects. Only Laura's growl. This is her standing up to Bob and her father for the first time. She uses all her power to walk out on her abuser. As she heads to school, the track "Birds in Hell" begins. Laura walks down the sidewalk as the audience sees shots of wires in the air and the asphalt is all around her. Laura goes to school as the clock spins backward and forward. She cries at her desk, unnoticed by Donna, the teacher, and the world. There is no need for dialogue on her last day; all the words have been spoken. Angelo Badalamenti and his

orchestrations have given the audience everything they need to know. Laura is just going through the motions, sleepwalking toward her destiny of death. "Birds in Hell" truly feels like a movement of classical music. It's one of the most beautiful pieces in the film, so of course we couldn't hear the entire track for twenty years.

"Birds in Hell" was put on the official soundtrack in a medley with three other songs. The medley, titled "Montage From Twin Peaks," is track eleven on the original soundtrack. It's paired with a song called "Girl Talk," which is used during the scene in which Donna and Laura talk about whether Mike could write a poem. (Answer: no.) Then the track fades to a portion of "Birds in Hell" for 1:18 before melding into "Laura Palmer's Theme" and finally "Falling." The full 4:20 version of "Birds in Hell" was not heard until 2011, when Lynch released the *Twin Peaks Archives*, one of the best gifts ever given to music fans: over two hundred previously unreleased MP3 tracks from the series and movie. One of those tracks was the extended "Birds in Hell." That is where the true beauty of the song can be heard. While I will always give Lynch/Frost a hard time for releasing and rereleasing the series on every platform again and again, I can't give them enough credit for releasing all of the music to fans. Too many great tracks were not released on the original soundtrack. The *FWWM* album has twelve tracks, and as I pointed out, forty-nine songs were used, so we needed this release to give us the full soundscape from the film. Now if we could get those tracks released on a vinyl box set, fans would really be happy. But my guess is they will just release the same three seasons again with one new bonus feature of how many doughnuts Agent Cooper eats in Season 1.

"MOVING THROUGH TIME"

This song has a repeated refrain performed on the vibes by Jay Hoggard that goes up and down, over and over for the entire 6:41 runtime. This gives us the feeling of being stuck in a time loop. While that spins obsessively, there is an acoustic bass played with a bow that moves back

and forth, hypnotizing the listener to sleep. On top of the arrangement is a piano played in the upper range that goes just where it wants, like a dreamer pointlessly walking through the clouds. "Moving Through Time" scores the scene in which Laura visits Bobby and goes through the motions of kissing him. She doesn't want his love or affection; she wants his drugs, to accelerate her numbness. She perfunctorily says goodnight to her mother for the last time and dresses in lingerie for her meeting with Leo. She plans to meet up with James, but she is just going through the motions, simply moving through time. The repetitive song stops when Laura stands to see the angel from the photo on the wall disappear before her eyes. Her destiny is set. As she wrote in her diary, according to Episode 16, "Tonight is the night that I die."

"HALF HEART"

The half-heart necklace was found in the pilot episode and is so associated with Laura Palmer that Lynch put her inside of one for the poster image. It was James who gave Laura the necklace, and in a really nice continuity touch, Lynch uses "Half Heart" twice, both times when James and Laura are together. The first time is when Laura meets James in what looks like a locker room at school. The song scores the classic line of dialogue "Gone like a turkey in the corn." (What would a Ryan Thanksgiving be without this line?) The second time is when Laura and James meet in the woods on the night she dies. Here, Laura whispers, "Let's get lost together," before she slaps him and says that his Laura disappeared. This second version has more of an echoed saxophone that plays the beautiful melody expressing the pain of this song.

The song itself has the typical *Twin Peaks* bass, but it does not bounce along. It's played much more slowly, for a more sensual feel. The saxophone plays a theme of longing filled with hope and desire. You can feel the saxophone calling out for something. It's very lonely for a love theme. We know that James and Laura's love affair is doomed, so it fits perfectly. The fact that it is called "Half Heart" and scores all of the James/Laura kissing scenes while being heartbreakingly sad makes it seem perfect for the two of them. Problem is this song was not written for the two of them.

The song was written as the love theme for the short-lived ABC series *On the Air*, which, comically, was hardly on the air at all. Seven episodes were produced; only three aired. Created by Frost/Lynch, it ran from June 20 to July 4, 1991. "Half Heart," despite being the theme of the James/Laura relationship, was never released until the Season 2 CD came out in 2007. But it was when the *Twin Peaks Archive* was released that I discovered this song is actually the love theme from *On the Air*. Lynch released three other versions of the song, which are not as full of longing as the one used in *FWWM*, but it is most certainly the same song. Since *FWWM* was filmed the same year that *On the Air* was broadcast, it made sense to use this track, since no one really saw the short-lived series. This song was too good for just one use.

"THE VOICE OF LOVE"

Before I cover this final song, I just want to point out that I could have picked any of the forty-nine tracks that were played in the film to focus on. I could write an entire book about the score Badalamenti wrote. I was hoping to interview him for the book. I must sadly tell this story. I did finally get to email him and ask him for an interview. He agreed and asked for my list of questions. I sent him twenty hard-core questions that I was so excited to get the answers to. (Example: You use a trumpet for the theme song and a saxophone for the scene where Ed and Norma are listening to the song on the radio. When you are scoring, how do you choose the main instrument? To you, what does the trumpet represent? And what does the saxophone represent?) I checked in with him six weeks later. He responded by saying that he was feeling too ill to do the interview. He thanked me for loving his music and hoped he would recover from his illness in time to be able to do the interview. He didn't. I had waited thirty years to get to talk to one of my musical mentors. It didn't happen. He also shares a birthday with Stephen Sondheim, which has always meant something to me, although I'm not sure what. I was so bummed that the interview couldn't happen, but then I remembered a part of our email exchange. Yes, I didn't get answers to my questions, but I did get to tell him something. In my email I said, "I am a piano player myself, and practicing 'Dance of The Dream Man' is what taught me how to strengthen my left hand. (I still struggle with that bass line.) Please consider making this fellow piano player's dream come true and let's do a deep dive into all the beautiful music you have created over the years. Thank you so much for all your music.

It has been the score for all my writing sessions." When he responded to cancel the interview he added, "I do so much appreciate that my music has been a source of inspiration for you. All the best and be well Scott. Angelo." I like to think that maybe my words of appreciation brought him a little bit of joy as he battled his illness. I may not have been able to get information *from* him, but I was able to get information *to* him, about how much his music shaped my life. I'll take it.

"The Voice of Love" ends the film. Laura has died. She sits in The Red Room with Agent Cooper standing by her side, his hand on her shoulder. She finally sees her angel, and Laura weeps with joy. Badalamenti was tasked with the assignment of writing a piece of music that would wash away all the pain that Laura and the audience had experienced. There are only three minutes between the end of the brutal train car death scene and the first notes of "The Voice of Love." Angelo Badalamenti had to take the audience from the deep despair of graphic violence to the highest depths of sweet forgiveness, love, and peace. Laura has suffered for over ninety straight minutes. I can't imagine sitting down and writing a piece of music that could wash that amount of pain away. Lucky for all of you, Lynch tasked Badalamenti with it and not me. He came back with a gorgeous piece of music.

> "David says, 'Angelo, there is gonna be an angel and tears coming out of [Laura's] eyes. As she is crying, I want everyone who sees it to cry and feel for her because everyone loves her.'"
>
> - Angelo Badalamenti, Criterion Blu-ray bonus feature

All of the music is created on keyboards. The chords meld, and the brightness of the tune is the first in the film. There is hope and love in each note as the chords blend together seamlessly. It has the melodrama of "Laura Palmer's Theme" without going over the top. The song never unfolds into a big moment. It just slowly builds.

"The Voice of Love" has no words in the film, but a year later, Julee Cruise sang the song with new lyrics written by Lynch to end her second album, of the same name. Lynch wrote the lyrics "Listen. Listen. I hear the voice of love." Julee sings it so sweetly. Laura gets her angel; we get our voice of love. The song and her second album didn't have the splash that Cruise's *Floating Into the Night* had. Julee Cruise is still sore about it. She told me, "I think a lot of people forgot about that entire song. Warner Bros. acted like they didn't know us. I am glad it is out there because it didn't get any attention before. People got sick of *Twin Peaks* real fast, and they [Warner Bros.] didn't support it."

Some may still not have heard Cruise's interpretation of the song, because it was never released on an official *Twin Peaks* soundtrack. I implore you to seek it out. It caps Laura's journey so well. I so wish that instead of having Julee Cruise sing "The World Spins" in *The Return*, Lynch would have had her do "The Voice of Love," since it connects to *FWWM*, and that part in *The Return* also is where they go back to the film. It would have been an interesting connection to The Angel and Laura Palmer, but here is another example where no one asked me. Shocking! I know.

Listed below are the songs in the order of how they play in the film, plus where they can be found. It is quite an investment to try to get all the songs and create your own complete soundtrack, but it's well worth it. Like all things *Twin Peaks*, it's not about going to just one place. You will need to purchase multiple albums to get them all, so you will wind up with repeat versions of some of the same songs.

THE *FWWM* SCORE IN ORDER

Theme from FWWM–Archive (saxophone, intro only)
Theme from FWWM–FWWM
Deer Meadow Shuffle**–(film version) TPS2
Mysterioso 1–Archive
Mysterioso 2–Archive
Teresa's Autopsy–Archive
Don't Do Anything (I Wouldn't Do)–FWWM
Mysterioso 2–(film version) Archive
Mysterioso–(film version) Archive
Dance of The Dream Man (solo sax)–Archive
Phillip Jeffries–Archive
Theme From FWWM–FWWM
Back to Fat Trout (Unease Motif_The Woods)–Archive
Twin Peaks Theme*–TPOS
The Bookhouse Boys–TPOS
Half Heart–TPS2
A Real Indication*–FWWM/Thought Gang
Girl Talk–FWWM/Archive
Laura Visits Harold–Archive

RR Swing**–Archive
The Black Dog Runs at Night*–FWWM/Thought Gang
Behind the Mask–Archive
Best Friends**–FWWM/Archive
Wash Your Hands–Archive
Distant Train–Archive
Laura Palmer's Theme (piano Tk3)–Archive
The Voice of Love (slow)–Archive
Laura's Dark Boogie–TPS2
The Pine Float–FWWM
Log Lady Presence–Archive
Questions in a World of Blue*–FWWM/The Voice of Love
(Vocals by Julee Cruise)
The Pink Room***–FWWM
Blue Frank***–TPS2
Dark Mood Woods–Archive
It's Your Father–Archive
Laura's Dark Boogie (clean)–Archive
Nightsea Wind–Archive
Laura Palmer's Theme–TPOS
Drug Deal Blues–TPS2
You Killed Mike/Night Bells (film mix)–Archive
James Visits Laura–Archive
Birds in Hell–Archive/FWWM
Moving Through Time–FWWM
Half Heart (solo)–Archive
Jacques's Cabin/The Train Car–Archive
Agnus Dei–Cherubini Requiem C-Moll****
Circumference of a Circle–Archive
Sycamore Trees (instrumental)–Archive
The Voice of Love (instrumental)–FWWM

Score by Angelo Badalamenti
* Written by David Lynch & Angelo Badalamenti
** Written by David Lynch & David Slusser
*** Written by David Lynch
**** Written by Luigi Cherubini

FWWM—The official soundtrack release
Twin Peaks Archive—The MP3 collection released by Davidlynch.com
Cherubini Requiem C-Moll—Ambrosian Singers & Philharmonia Orchestra Riccardo Muti
TPS2—The Official Season 2 and More
TPOS—*Twin Peaks Original Soundtrack*
Thought Gang—A side Lynch/Badalamenti album
The Voice of Love—Julee Cruise solo album

Special thanks to Ross Dudle

CHAPTER 7

Give Ron Garcia the Glad Hand

Ron Garcia, ASC (American Society of Cinematographers), may have been to one of their meetings, but only because he was forced. He was the director of photography for the pilot of *Twin Peaks* as well as *FWWM*. He unabashedly admits he was not a David Lynch fan when he took the first meeting for *Twin Peaks*. Ron Garcia's agent, Scott Harris, sent him the script of the pilot; Ron read it and threw it in the trash. He describes *Blue Velvet* as "not my cup of tea." His agent said, "You have to take an interview with David Lynch." Ron followed the rules of Hollywood, and meeting Lynch changed his mind. He said, "David was like a Jimmy Stewart/Boy Scout master. He was very focused, and I liked him as a person. He was first an artist and then became a filmmaker."

In the end, the script he tossed got tossed by Mark Frost and David Lynch as well. Garcia explained that they rewrote that first script, and that changed everything for him as well. Garcia said yes to the job and set television on a new path. He was there for the first filming of The Red Room, which was included in the European ending, developing the camera technique for capturing the action backward. He came up with the lighting and "warmth" look of the pilot. He was the one who photographed the fan in the Palmer house, shot all of the Snoqualmie Valley "mood" shots used as the transitions in the pilot, and put in motion the capturing of the hanging stoplight, the wind blowing through the trees, and (I'm saying it again because it's *that* big of a deal) the spinning fan in the Palmer house. All of that was Ron Garcia. So much of what is remembered from that pilot came from his eye. He passed on doing the series, but returned to the scene of the crime to photograph *FWWM*.

Ron Garcia again brought his unique eye to the screen. It was Garcia who asked Lynch if he could stay late (after twelve hours of shooting) to set up the shot of all the cigarette butts, bottles, and trash on the floor of The Pink Room. He was pleased when Lynch's final cut used that shot, which fades to the trees swaying in the mountains, a shot captured by Sean Doyle, the A camera operator. Garcia's contribution to the world of *Twin Peaks* can't be overstated. While I could have interviewed him about a million things, I focused on several specific shots. Ron talks as a professional should, using craft-based lingo. Hearing an experienced craftsman describe his craft is a reminder that there are still true experts in this world of mediocrity. I emailed him the following screen grabs, and we discussed the scenes over the phone in two sessions in 2021.

Scott Ryan: There are three lamps in the Palmer living room. You have a light just over Laura's head that makes her almost look like she has a halo. There's a lamp directly behind her and others on each side of the room. What's it like to shoot in a real house and use those lights to light it?

Ron Garcia: That light would've been hard to get on Kodak film. We shot this on Fuji film, which was ASA 500 forced developed to 1,000 ASA. That is how we could do this kind of lighting and get that kind of color out of it. Those are practical lamps with dimmers. The only difference is that I have an augmented light on Laura's face coming from the left to light her—soft. It had to be a little lower because Laura was getting pretty tired at this point in the film. She had a lot of dark circles under her eyes, and the makeup people were great and helped me out. Two lamps are practical and are lighting the walls. You can see on the ceiling there is one way in the corner behind the tree; that's just a small PAR can light down on the ground behind the pot that shoots up.

I did a lot of underneath lighting like that because my whole concept was that everything had to look like natural lighting—not movie lighting. This was a practical house, not a set. Here's Laura, who's going around doing all this cocaine, and Donna's just following her around like a puppy dog. We have the warmth of that house, the bucolic Seattle, woodsy house, warm and cozy, which is contradicting Laura's personality here. David's theory is that you go into a small town and you think everything is perfect, and then there's just chaos, drugs, and evil entities going through wires and telephone poles. There is rape and incest. So I kind of went for the opposite juxtaposition. We wanted to keep it warm in the shadows.

If you get too many warm lights, and with the filters in the camera, then everybody starts going orange. When I'm looking at Sheryl Lee, she's almost orange, which is really difficult for television because of the way they transferred it. In the feature, there was no problem, but as far as the pilot of *Twin Peaks* was concerned, I think it was way too orange. I remember after I shot the pilot, I didn't think I was going to work again in the film industry. I didn't like what the pilot looked like from the telecine dailies, but the CFI [Consolidated Film Industries] lab saved my coloring, and it became what it is now.

Ryan: It's often picked as one of the best pilots in television history, so I think you might be able to keep your job. The color is so amazing, with the lights in the background and the liquor bottles up front. Is it hard to keep all of that in focus?

Garcia: When I first met David, for the television pilot, he wanted wide angles. He wanted to see the environment, which I loved. That's where we hit it off. Long lenses are great for cop shows, but for storytelling? Wide. The bottles are actually out of focus. Sheryl's focus is spot-on her eyes. It was shot with a 21 mm prime Panavision lens, rather than a zoom lens. That keeps everything in focus. I'm a diffusion guy. Moira Kelly is soft. So this particular still that you grabbed, the assistant is racking that focus back and forth between actresses for their dialogue. This is one of my favorite scenes, when Moira says, "Aren't you gonna fix me a drink?" Sheryl turns around and gives her the stink eye. I loved it. I worked with Moira when I did the first year of the reboot of *Hawaii Five-O*. She had grown up, had kids, and was still one of the nicest people.

Ryan: In Laura's dream sequence, the camera goes from room to room, and the picture on Laura's wall comes to life. How the heck did you do that?

Garcia: It looks relatively simple, but it wasn't. We dollied toward Frances Bay, and we had to make these hard right angles as we went through that door, without causing shadows of the camera operator sitting on the peewee dolly, the first assistant cameraman, and the dolly grip. So three people had to fit through with no shadows.

Ryan: It looks like one take to me.

Garcia: It is. I love those kinds of shots, where it challenges you to get through a space where you didn't think the camera and a dolly could get through. Before Steadicam, we were all trained that you could only go so far with a camera and there always had to be a cut. Hitchcock took care of that in *Rope*, where there's ten cuts in the entire feature. Patricia Norris, the production designer, and I talked about this. David and her wanted the camera to go through a real narrow passageway. The set had to match the photograph on the wall in her bedroom. I'm trying to remember how I got rid of the shadows. I think I dimmed the lights down so that when I got close to the wall you wouldn't see Frances's shadow. This was shot on film. Today, with digital, there would be no problem.

Ryan: This is at the end, when Laura sees The Angel. I was just curious about the lighting in this one, because you can see almost a blue spotlight on her face. I love this shot.

Garcia: Oh, thank you. I lit her with a special still strobe light. At that time I was able to sync the strobe light to the camera shutter to make it feel like a fixed light that was not strobing. It was at 6,500 kelvin, which is a blue light. I don't see the strobe light in the shot of Laura's close-up, but it was blue, just like the blue cast around Laura with The Angel. The Angel was lit with the same strobe light, but I don't believe it was strobing on The Angel. It might've been. We used a lot of strobe light.

Ryan: In the shooting script, there is no mention of an angel. Do you remember if The Angel was something that David added on the set?

Garcia: I remember it was at the end of the shooting schedule, back in LA, that we shot all of The Red Room. I remember shooting The Angel. There were a lot of ideas that David tried to do. We, of course, suspended her, hung her in the air, then shot her at different angles, and then he dissolved the one he liked. When The Angel appears, that's an optical; that angel wasn't there, because he didn't want to do a wire removal in post. But it's kind of a repose from the train car, when Ronette gets an angel in that scene. I put the same light on that angel there, knowing that David was going to somehow put them all together and use a dissolve.

The first I remember talking about The Angel was in Laura's bedroom, because Patty Norris had the picture of the kids. I had talked to David about doing the effect where the angel disappears from the photo on her wall. I was really into Photoshop at that time. I mentioned if he

Before and after views of the angel in the photo on Laura's wall.
Photo courtesy of New Line Cinema

took that photo on the wall, he could remove the angel and do a simple dissolve. David liked the idea. My two cents is that Laura is dying, and her angel is going to disappear. This is what is unique about David. He takes everything that everyone says in his environment. When he is directing, he goes with the flow. He has one foot in reality and the other in his subconscious all the time. That is focus. That is hard to do. He takes symbols while he is shooting and incorporates it or moves on. That taught me an awful lot when I am lighting or directing. I might have a plan going in, but don't stick to it.

Ryan: Tell me about filming in The Pink Room? Did he really play that music while you were shooting it?

Garcia: Yes, very loud. We were in there for twelve hours with that driving music. It drove me crazy! The more we were there, I started getting influenced by that music, and it helped me block the lenses and the movement on that scene. I articulated the top lights to the music. I had a canvas roof that Patty Norris built for me. Then I stuck these PAR cans in it. It was just stage lights with red and blue pounding down. David liked the strobes that I picked for The Pink Room. I pulsed the lights. So I used the strobes from The Pink Room again in The Red Room with The Angel.

Ryan: You had a lot going on in The Room Above the Convenience

Ron Garcia is on set with Sheryl Lee, Jonny Leppell, and Frances Bay.
Photo courtesy of New Line Cinema

Store. [For the rest of the interview we will print this as TRATCS]. This scene changes a lot between the film version and the extended version in the *Missing Pieces*. Did you suspect the movie was going to be too long?

Garcia: We shot over a million feet of film in forty-six days. I broke it down this morning over coffee, and that means twenty-one thousand feet of film a day. With two cameras, that is eleven hours a day of the camera running. If it was a fourteen-hour day; that only leaves three hours for makeup, rehearsal, and lighting. I was running and gunning. It was faster than any TV show I ever shot, and it was a feature! David didn't have a lot of money, and we had to boogie. Look at the *Missing Pieces*; there is a lot of stuff they cut out. I think Mary Sweeney's first cut was three and half hours long. I can't believe they cut out scenes with David Bowie. There was the whole thing in the hallway with an explosion. They blackened the wall of some old hotel in Seattle, Washington. David Bowie was supposed to walk through a different set before he landed on the stairs, and we were gonna use that set I was designing twice, once for when David Bowie goes there and once for when Bob and MFAP get to the TRATCS. But the set got cut because they didn't have the money to build it without opticals.

Ryan: I would have loved to see them connect David Bowie's appearance in the FBI office and the hotel with how Bob and MFAP get into that room.

Garcia: They blackened the wall of the hotel, and then they had to redo it. It was going to match something that never happened. David Bowie walks in and asks for a room. It goes to him coming down the stairs, and there is an explosion, and then there are guests in that hallway looking at him. Then he was supposed to disappear, and cut to the electrical power where the power of Bob comes through, and reappear as he walks in the FBI office; that is why he is walking strangely. In Lynch's eye, the energy in the wires that transferred him from Buenos Aires to the FBI office blew up on Bowie. There was a glitch during the transfer through the telephone wires. Then he reappeared back in Buenos Aires and then disappeared again.

I designed a set, which was never used, to give him ideas of what I could do in camera instead of visual F/X. Just like in the beginning of Laura's dream that we talked about, with Frances Bay, Bowie was supposed to come through that door, we would see her grandson standing there in a vortex, and then the kid walked over and sat on the couch. It was supposed to come into TRATCS. In that corner was supposed to be a red, smoky vortex, and as the camera dollied around that darkened door, in one part of the wall we would see a glowing vortex and the camera goes through and Bob and MFAP walk into the room. This was a transition that Lynch was trying to work out. Then Bob sits down at the table, and then we cut to the wide shot of all of them. David Bowie wasn't in it. It was a totally different scene, but we never shot it. The set I was supposed to design was supposed to be able to do that in real time. If that makes sense?

Ryan: It does, but only because I am crazy. There are a few times in the movie where Lynch uses the same scenes over again, like "Is this future or is this past?" It sounds like he wanted to introduce Laura's dream and Agent Jeffries in TRATCS the same way, both starting with Mrs. Tremond inviting them through the same door. Laura goes one way, to see Cooper, MFAP, and the ring. Jeffries goes through the vortex into TRATCS and attends one of their meetings. That would have been so cool, because it opens the idea that maybe Mrs. Tremond gave Jeffries a painting for his wall as well. I love this. I wish it would have been shot. Tell me about filming in TRATCS.

Garcia: On this still, the gentleman in the red knit hat is Jürgen Prochnow from *Das Boot*. We actually used his mouth in the shot down the throat with the tonsils, when Bob screams at Laura in her room. David bought a full pig's head from the butcher, cut off at the neck. He opened the pig's mouth and kept it open. There was a lens that could attach to my motion picture camera, and it was long and had a light on it, and it went into the camera lens. It was an endoscope. It was a medical camera that I rented. I showed it to David. He wanted to cut to a close-up of the pig's mouth that was lit by the lens itself. We dollied out of the pig's shot, and it went into The Jumping Man. We shot Jürgen's mouth, and he was screaming, and we dollied out like we did with the pig. I don't think he ever used the pig, because David liked that you can see the tonsils, and pigs don't have the tonsil.

Ryan: "Pigs don't have the tonsil" is the best title for this interview or any interview. TRATCS is lit really strangely. How did you achieve that?

Garcia: It was hard to set up all the lights in that set. I spent two hours lighting it, which was the longest it took on the film, and then we shot it

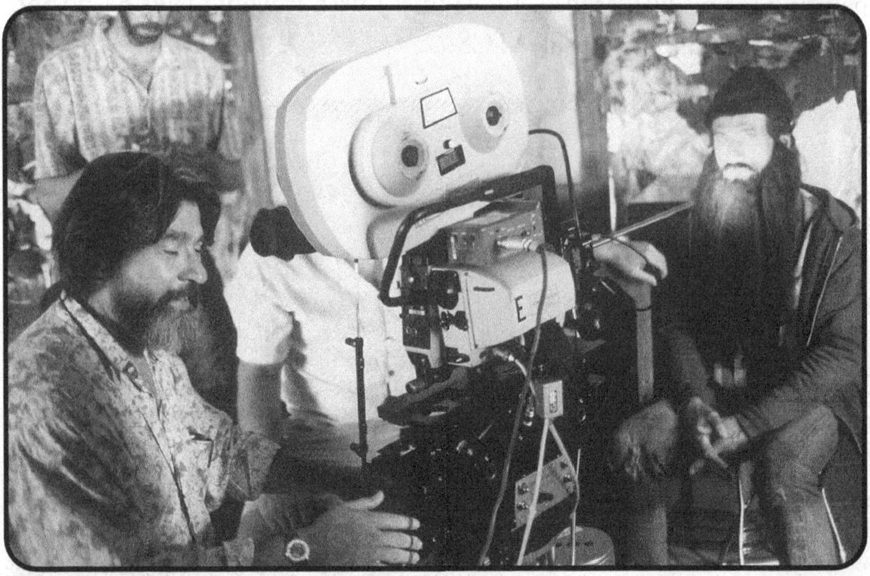

Ron Garcia is behind the camera; note that on the other end is the endoscope that captured Jürgen Prochnow's tonsil. Photo courtesy of New Line Cinema

all in one to catch up. I was running all those flashes and lights at 3000 ASA, I don't think too many people pushed it that much. It allowed me to shoot film cameras that can blank out when you use a strobe. But in TRATCS I used an electronic box between the strobes and the film camera, and I synced up the shutters with the strobe so that it was strobing with the shutter open. What that did was give me control where I could not have the flash. I didn't want it to be like The Pink Room. It gave me a huge range to make it feel a little different. It went by the wayside when it got transferred to digital, but you can feel it in a projection in a darkened theater on 35 mm.

Ryan: I saw the film in 35 mm recently and I felt like it was better than the Blu-ray release, and now I know why. Thanks for that. Our next picture is of Bobby and Laura in the woods. This scene is so dark; how did you light this one?

Garcia: This is an amazing scene with Sheryl and how she could giggle like that. It's so different from her other scenes. David and I got into an artist debate about this shot. David wanted it DARK. It was nighttime. I thought I would make it "movie dark" and let the audience see the surrounding area. I think I had four 1200K HMI lamps and bounced them off four-by-four white foam core bounce boards for fill. We do the rehearsal, and it's pitch-black outside. David said, "Ron, it's so bright here." I said, "David, that is because you are looking at the lights. Look at the actors." He said, "No, it's just supposed to be lit by the deputy's flashlight." I think I was just ornery that night. I said, "Do you want to burden the actors with having to light the scenes with their flashlights and have to light the person who is talking?" We went back and forth. I took three of the HMI lights out, and he said it was still too bright. He could tell I was a little miffed. I took one of the lights and bounced it off a silver tip tree where I had a light bouncing off the needles of a pine tree. I got just enough to be sure I wouldn't get too much grain on the film. He looked at me and said, "Where is that light coming from to light Laura and Bobby?" I thought about it for a second and I said, "David, it's from the same place the music is coming from." He clammed up, and I got to keep that light on. We were lucky it worked and didn't have to shoot it again.

Ryan: Moving on to the couch scene. On this one, you start way up, and the scene ends very close to Laura's face. This is one of my favorite shots in the film, because to me it tells the whole story. Her destiny cannot be avoided, no matter what happens. When you get so close to someone's face, what are the challenges?

Garcia: When I saw the rehearsal, David placed them like that. I thought the best way to start the scene, psychologically, is to have her being looked at by The Angel, but when you get closer to her, she has been totally destroyed by her father and Bob. Here is a normal place—cozy, warm. Patty might have brought that rug in. David picked beautiful outfits for the girls, and their makeup is perfect. You see them as normal teenagers hanging out. The way to express that is to film it from up and looking down. David liked that idea. This is another practical set, and it had high ceilings. I think that is a 14 mm lens, where everything is in focus. By the time you get in close to Laura, you can see her soul in this shot. It isn't my photography; it's Sheryl Lee. When she says the dialogue "And the angels wouldn't help you because they've all gone away," to me she is talking about her death. She is this beautiful young woman wishing for an angel to save her. This is all Sheryl. I put hard lights on the side to create the shadows for the tables in the high shot. I didn't change the lighting very much for the close-up. If it takes too long to light, you lose the actor. I just put some double-diffusion paper over the hard light coming from the left on the wide shot, and she was lit. I learned to shape faces without taking time. You can see in her eyes there are only two lights hitting her. See the two little dots under her pupils?

Ryan: Oh wow, I do! I have seen this a million times and never noticed that.

Garcia: What you are seeing are four-by-four pieces of diffusion. I like to see a light dot in their eyes to show them off. If she was standing, those two little dots would be in the black part of her eye. To me, it's not sexy, the way they were dressed; it was natural, and Donna and Laura were the yin and yang. There is Laura, who has all this internal strife, and we are inside her head. They are innocent, but not. Donna wants to be just like Laura. She's just as sexy and just as beautiful, but just hasn't gotten there yet. I think a lot of people identify with the Donna character.

The Donna [Lara Flynn Boyle] from the pilot didn't have the depth at that time that this one [Moira Kelly] did. Sheryl Lee was in the pilot, but she was dead, wrapped up in plastic the entire shoot. I mean, she was sweet and stuff, but she was in and out. I didn't have a clue at the depth of her acting ability until I saw what she did in *FWWM*.

Ryan: In the train car there is so much going on with lighting. I love how there is light and darkness throughout this scene. The light on the floor is incredible. How was filming that scene?

Garcia: That's when I got the most upset and was hoping Sheryl was OK, when she looks into the mirror in the dilapidated Pullman car.

Ryan: Why did you get upset?

Her performance—she was out there. I mean, that was a powerful scene, when she's about to die. She *knew* she was gonna die. She is looking up and sees her father, and sees Bob, then her father, and looking in the mirror; that was just the most torturous. I was so busy lighting it and doing all the mechanical things. We shot a lot of film, very fast. She had so much to go through! When I saw it cut together, it really upset me. It really hit a visceral, psychological shadow of my psyche. Just the horror of someone who's not only being accosted by her father and this ghost out of the electricity that David developed, but it's kind of like we have this shadow, this evil. We have good in us, where the archetypes of God and the Devil are basically archetypes. They have to be together, but we deny the Devil in us, the shadow, dark, deep stuff of us, and we always go for the goodness and the fantasy of "We're all good." That's not what happens in the psyche. We're both good and evil, and David—when he's doing his work and his paintings—he gets down there. He does Transcendental Meditation, so you do get in contact with David's dark shadow.

I was really worried about Sheryl at the end of that day of shooting. It was a really long day. I think we changed the schedule after this scene, because she went out there into that shadow side of herself, and it affected me, because I lived with her on the set and watched her *be* in that torment all the time. I was really concerned about her. But not while I was shooting; it was after the filming that I was hoping she was OK . . . much later. Because it's like post-traumatic syndrome. She went out there and was crazy; that came from deep inside of her. That's what got to me.

Ryan: It doesn't surprise me that you felt that way watching her do that in person, because I felt it watching it on film. I am forever moved by what she did.

Garcia: Everyone on set was really *looking* at her—the focus puller, the camera operator, the gaffer, me—we started to worry about her. Some of us asked, "Are you OK? Do you need a break?" And she said, "No, no, no," and she just dove in. She was one of the bravest actors I've ever seen, to keep that pace and that kind of work. Acting is internal work; it's a lot of energy to lose yourself and become a character, but also be able to hang onto yourself at the same time. She damn near lost herself.

Toward the end of the schedule, I started getting really depressed. I just felt concern for everybody, including *me*. I was thinking, "This is really affecting all of us." It almost felt like psychological gratuitous violence. I couldn't watch the film afterward, when it was cut together. I went to the screening, but I didn't watch the film. I put so much effort into my photography and tried to give David what he wanted; then I looked at all the amount of mental work we had to do to achieve that. I was just photographing it. Sheryl had to stay in that moment and keep that tone going—David's tone of *FWWM*—and I started feeling like I was doing *Blue Velvet*, which I didn't like.

Ten years later, when I sat down and was away from it long enough, I thought it was one of the most antidrug films ever made. When I finally looked at it objectively, I think it perfectly displays mental violence with the relationship between Laura, Bob, and her dad. It became a brilliant film to me, and then I started realizing why David's *Twin Peaks* hit a lot of psyche in our culture. It got booed at Cannes because it wasn't like anything even the Europeans had seen. And it was a different kind of violence; it was psychological violence, and you're inside her head. That's where David went to, inside his head, and transferred that over to Sheryl Lee.

And she nailed it.

Sheryl Lee signed this photo of Laura Palmer in The Red Room for Ron Garcia. Photo courtesy of Ron Garcia

CHAPTER 8

What You Are About to Read Are Missing Pieces

As I have stated, being a *Twin Peaks* fan has never been easy. In fact, if you looked at it objectively, it really seems like the suits did everything they could to make sure no one was a fan of *Twin Peaks*. They moved the series around on the ABC schedule. *FWWM* played for only a week or two, then it all but disappeared. The pilot of *Twin Peaks* was insanely never released on video until 2007. (That is seventeen Bob damn years after it aired!) Only the first seven episodes (minus the pilot) were released on VHS in the last week of September 1991. I know this because I still have the check stub on which the purchase was subtracted from my pay, dated September 26, 1991, from the video store where I worked. (Yes, the same video store that two years later I would steal *FWWM* from. I'm currently out on bail awaiting trial from my confession in Chapter 5.) I paid $75.81 for those seven episodes. That was the wholesale price, so the list price was probably closer to $150. It was a good thing I was an employee so that I could afford it with my discount, because all I got paid after the purchase was $14. So I couldn't eat that week? Who cared! I owned seven episodes of my beloved series. But how was anyone going to become a new fan of the series when it didn't start at the beginning and it ended with Agent Cooper getting shot and that was it? There was no YouTube on which to watch bootleg copies of the series. There was no video on the internet in 1991. It would have taken four days to just download the opening credits with AOL dial-up.

The European pilot was released on VHS, but that wasn't going to help bring in new fans, because that includes a closed ending that makes no sense if you continue on with the series. It ends with Bob, as an actual person, being shot and killed. So why would you continue on to the next episode, where Cooper doesn't know who did it? He had just watched the killer get shot. Today we can argue about what to call *The Return*, or what Part 8 means, but back in the early nineties you couldn't even find the series to argue about it. So it wasn't like the fan base could grow and make *FWWM* a hot property when it was released in theaters.

I was fortunate to work at Video Time during the run of *Twin Peaks.* On the following pages I have scanned some of the cool things I "acquired" while working there. One of my favorites is a counter standee that had red curtains with the Red Room floor (properly done in cream and maroon, not black and white), which could be pulled on the ends to reveal Laura Palmer in the heart necklace with *Fire Walk With Me* revealed under her. It was like a pop-up book for obsessive fans like me. That standee never made it to the counter of Video Time. It was unpacked and taken to my car faster than MFAP can suck creamed corn off a spoon backward. I also kept all the ads that were sent trying to convince local video stores to buy the film. If a store bought a four-pack (for the low price of $275), it also got a shirt, a coffee thermos, and a red coffee cup with the *FWWM* logo.

I have had these items (except the shirt, which the owners wouldn't give me. Why? They didn't know I was stealing all the other stuff, so they had no real reason to withhold it from me) all these years, but I didn't drink out of the thermos until 2020, during a lockdown live Facebook event. I thought it would be fun. It was not. The inside of the thermos smelled like scorched engine oil, and it made the coffee taste like it had a fish in it. But I have decided that on August 28, 2022, I will drink from the ceramic coffee cup for the first time. I'll let you know on Twitter how that goes. I don't know what I am saving all this stuff for. It's been thirty years. It's probably time. The picture with the blue rose and tape recorder

MY VIDEO STORE COLLECTION

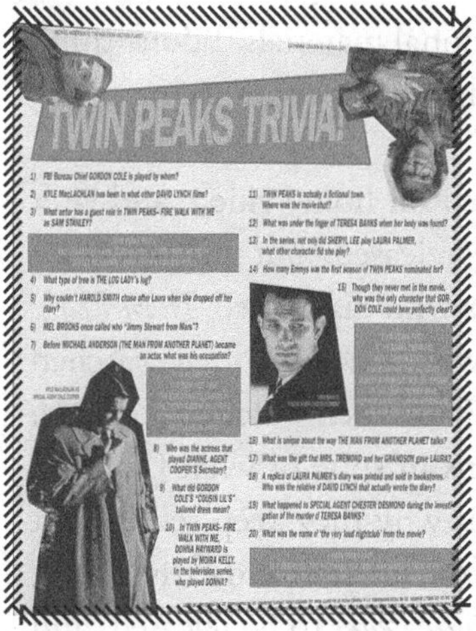

On the previous page is a two page pull out with all the reasons for video stories to rent *FWWM* on VHS. The VHS was not available as a direct sale to the public. Below that is the counter standee, and behind it are the thermos and red *FWWM* coffee cup.

Above are the trivia questions and diner promo picture, which has a blue rose and a piece of pie on the counter. Below is my VHS box set for the first seven episodes of the series. It took 80 percent of my paycheck, but I was twenty-two, and who needed money when you had part of the series?

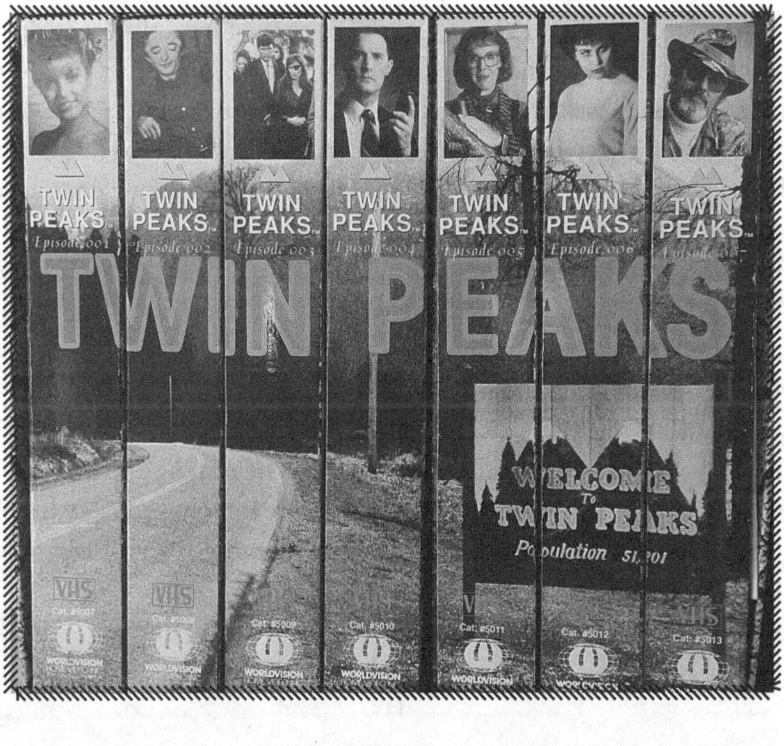

was a trivia sheet that came with the promotional materials. I don't think I have seen these promos show up online. I hope you enjoy seeing them, maybe for the first time.

On January 6, 1993, *FWWM* was released on home video, and later a VHS box set of both seasons would be released, but still no pilot episode. I have met many fans over the years who discovered *Twin Peaks* by watching it out of order. Some started with *FWWM*, then watched the episodes. Some started with Episodes 1-7 and then watched *FWWM*. Yikes. Somehow, the series amassed new fans in spite of what CBS did with the cockamamie releases. Maybe that is why they keep releasing it now, to try to make up for it. But for most of the nineties and early 2000s, there just wasn't any hope for new or old *Twin Peaks* to be released, and there wasn't much coverage of the series outside of *Wrapped in Plastic*. But there was a holy grail for crazy fans like me—the deleted scenes from *FWWM*. I bring up the previous home release history just to set the stage for the battle for the deleted scenes. *Twin Peaks* fans have suffered from the very beginning. There wasn't a lot of information about these deleted scenes, like whether they even existed. There were just questions. If there really were missing scenes, what were they? Where were they? Who owned them? And who really pulled the trigger on JFK?

When Bob Engels and David Lynch wrote the film script, they did so thinking it would be a "normal" episode of *Twin Peaks* in that it would include the entire cast from the television series. Engels said, "We would try to think of how to get every regular in it. We wanted to know what each character would be up to." An early draft was about 180 pages, according to Engels. The shooting script was 126 pages, with Lynch improvising some extra scenes during the shoot. When they got into the editing room, they realized the first cut was way too long. I have been told by those I have interviewed over the years that the first cut was anywhere from three and half to five hours plus. Engels said Lynch was surprised when the studio wasn't all-in for an extended film. He said, "We joked about it being really long, and Lynch's response was to put an intermission in it. I think it was New Line Cinema that probably flipped out at the length. That was not good. It is just the basics of the movie business. So businesswise put an end to that idea."

So if *Twin Peaks* was a dying franchise in the early nineties, how did we know there were deleted scenes? We have the Japanese to thank for that. *Twin Peaks* was more popular in Japan than it was in America. Matthew Jackson reported in a 2017 article on Mentalfloss.com, "*Fire Walk With Me* premiered there in May of 1992, well before it got an American release, and ran in Japanese theaters all through the summer." Those showings came with a program that had pictures from scenes that were not in the movie. Here are two pictures from that program, courtesy of John Thorne.

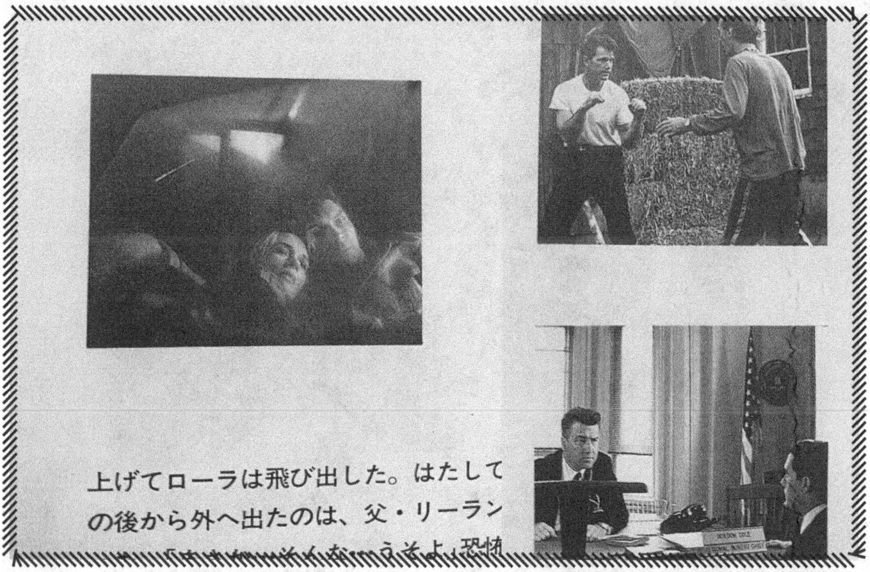

The photos that started the discussion were of Norma and Big Ed in a parked car and Agent Desmond fighting Sheriff Cable. These were pictures from scenes that were not in the film. Big Ed (Everett McGill) wasn't in the released film at all. That was quite a revelation. In Poland, a lobby card had a picture of Leland Palmer from the scene in which he says he is hungry. Three clues out there across the globe. That was all there was. But it was enough to keep fans talking on the Dugpa message board. (We didn't have Facebook comments; we had message boards, and that's all we needed.)

Brian Kursar (Dugpa website, coproducer of the *Missing Pieces*): The cover story by Tim Lucas in the March/April 1993 issue of *Video Watchdog (#16)* really lit the fire. *Video Watchdog* urged fans to write

The fight scene from the film was reenacted by Josh Eisenstadt and me in front of Sheriff Cable (Gary Bullock) at the Twin Peaks Festival in 2016. Photos courtesy of New Line Cinema, Lynn Groves, and Heather Bruce in to show their support of the release of the scenes, hopefully on a laser disc format, as DVD was not yet a reality.

New Line Cinema had caught wind of the interest, citing that it was the most popular catalog-title request in their entire back catalog. In early 1999, New Line engaged Lynch to work on a special edition of the film. In November of 1999, New Line prematurely announced the inclusion of deleted scenes, only to retract the announcement shortly thereafter. In the months (years?) to follow, things seemed bleak, and at one point the studio confirmed their decision to release the DVD without the mythical deleted scenes, citing "rights issues."

Fans that got wind of this began petitioning for the release. A website run by Jordan Chambers called the *Twin Peaks Gazette* ran a campaign called Operation Creamed Corn. This campaign urged fans to send letters and cans of creamed corn to the movie studio to help urge the studio to rethink releasing a bare-bones DVD.

New Line got the message and decided to delay the release to try and restart negotiations with the French rights holders. The delay lasted a full two years. At one point, New Line contacted me and asked that fans stop sending cans of creamed corn, as this was around the time of the 2001 anthrax scare, and one of the packages containing creamed corn had burst, with the creamed corn leaking out of the package. This package triggered a lockdown of the New Line office. Talk about pain and sorrow. Sadly, due to challenges with negotiations and timing of Lynch's availability, New Line decided to release the DVD shortly thereafter.

Actor Gary Bullock, who played Sheriff Cable, appeared at the then fan-run Twin Peaks Festival in 2002 and showed slides from his fight scene with Chris Isaak that had been given to him by Lynch. That confirmed that the scene wasn't just written in the script or that the photo from the Japanese program wasn't simply a publicity shot. Bullock confirmed that the scene was in fact *filmed*.

Over the following years, rumors circulated that the deleted scenes would be released, but it didn't happen. The same year that Bullock gave the slideshow, the film was released on DVD for the first time. No deleted scenes were included. The trail was cold again. It would be reported over and over again that talks had fallen through with MK2, the company that owned the scenes, or that CBS didn't want to pay for rights. It seemed the deleted scenes would never see the light of day.

Brian Kursar: Lynch would only complete the scenes if he could remaster, edit, and score the scenes to match the same quality of the theatrical cut. The scenes needed to live in the same world as the movie. New Line and MK2, the company that owned the scenes, were unable to figure out a way to make it financially viable to do so. Keep in mind, this is an older film, and pulling the film negative from a vault, transferring it, editing, and scoring it isn't trivial, and the costs were huge. There was one person, however, who was able to figure out how to make it work. His name was Ken Ross, who at the time was the vice president of CBS Home Entertainment. Hot on the heels of the massive success of the 2007 *Twin Peaks Definitive Gold Box* set, Ken was looking for ideas for extras should they do a follow-up Blu-ray box set. By chance, he had found my site and contacted me. After a number of phone calls, and a bit of help from documentary producer Charles de Lauzirika, we were able to convince Ken that if there was one thing that would justify a *Twin Peaks* fan to purchase a new box set, it was the inclusion of the mythical deleted scenes.

I can say without any hesitation that if it weren't for Ken Ross, the *Missing Pieces* would still be missing. To make the release financially viable, he would need to not only secure the rights for the scenes from MK2, but also secure the rights for distribution globally and have it all line up with Lynch's schedule. Now, what people don't know is that this was a very complicated negotiation between multiple companies across the globe that took six years to complete. I've never seen such passion and commitment from anyone in the home entertainment industry to make something like this happen. The success of that box set release helped pave the way for *The Return*, and both would not have happened without the powerhouse that is Ken Ross.

In 2014, those scenes, most of them containing members of the original cast of the series, were released on the Blu-ray with the ironic title *Twin*

Peaks: The Entire Mystery. (One of my favorite things ever is that Lynch and Frost approved this release with that title WHILE they were writing *The Return*, knowing that box would, in fact, not contain the *entire* mystery. Classic *Twin Peaks*.) This was the first time the deleted scenes were revealed outside of the leaked script that had floated across the internet (and in used-CD stores) for years. Everyone expected to see the three scenes they knew about from the photos, but there were plenty of surprises. On the day it was released, I took a half day off from work and sat in a chair by my mailbox waiting for it to arrive. Popping in that disk was like achieving a dream I had harbored most of my life. The scenes didn't disappoint. They exceeded my expectations. It was a surprise to me that they were edited together as a feature film. These had never been thought of as the *MISSING PIECES*, which is how we all refer to them now. They were just deleted scenes, nothing more. But they were so, so much more.

The most shocking part to me was that Lynch actually did film scenes that took place *after* the series finale. Lynch had filmed that scripted ending of Annie Blackburn in the hospital, as well as Doc Hayward and Sheriff Truman talking to Cooper after he had smashed the mirror. Good Cooper was seen in The Red Room. This was new *Twin Peaks*, moving the story forward.

For my first viewing, I watched them alone. I soaked in the feeling of getting to see characters and actors who had meant so much to me in my youth. I don't know how other "original" *Twin Peaks* fans feel, but for me, watching the *Missing Pieces* was more emotional and more rewarding than watching *The Return*. In these scenes, the actors hadn't aged. They were still the characters exactly as I remembered them. Also, they behaved like their *Twin Peaks* characters. By the time Frost and Lynch were writing *The Return*, they were so hell-bent on not leaning into any nostalgia that they gave fans nothing to connect to the original series. That is not a slam on *The Return*. I enjoyed it, but it didn't soothe my pure-fan longing for a true return to the town of Twin Peaks like the *Missing Pieces* did. It was emotional to see Don Davis with Charlotte Stewart again. It was incredible to hear Jack Nance's unique readings on lines like "You couldn't build a decent doghouse with it." You actually got to see Agent Cooper in scenes you hadn't seen before. The Agent

Cooper we knew. The one we loved. Dougie Jones is a hoot, but he ain't Coop. Now, before you set fire to this book, unfollow me on Twitter, and unsubscribe to *The Blue Rose*, I like *The Return*, but purely in terms of returning to my *Twin Peaks*, nothing can top that feeling of watching the *Missing Pieces* for the first time.

The more I thought about my first feelings, the more I wanted to know what others thought. I decided to ask four longtime fans who, to me, are the pinnacle of *Twin Peaks* fans and scholars.

Brad Dukes (author of *Reflections: An Oral History of Twin Peaks*): The *Missing Pieces* were and still are a dream to me. Like they don't exist on a DVD sitting on my shelf that I can watch at any time I choose. For years, I read the *Fire Walk With Me* shooting script and put faces and voices to the action. It seemed too good to be true that we would someday see the tiniest peek at "Dopple Cooper" after Episode 29 or more of David Bowie as Agent Jeffries. When I saw those moving images for the first time, I was floored. For years I wanted a third season of *Twin Peaks*, but after I saw *The Return,* I realized I wanted the Season 3 that would have happened in 1991. Frank Silva, Don Davis, Jack Nance, and so many others had more work to do in *Twin Peaks*. The *Missing Pieces* is a true blessing in that sense, giving my dream and those characters a few more minutes before I wake up.

Mary Hütter (appeared in the *Twin Peaks Definitive Gold Box* bonus features and is a contributor to *The Blue Rose*): I think I may have enjoyed *The Return* way more if I hadn't seen the *Missing Pieces*. Starting with the rerelease of *The Secret Diary of Laura Palmer*, the release of the Season 2 soundtrack, and *Twin Peaks Music Archive*, the late aughts/early teens were a nostalgic euphoria for original *Twin Peaks* fans. The *Missing Pieces* were the crowning jewel, because of how long we'd been asking and yearning for them. They were aptly named, because when I was finally able to see them, the *Missing Pieces* seemed to fill little cracks in me that I didn't even realize were there. It was the feeling of seeing a loved one you hadn't seen in years and suddenly they were right there hugging you. My extended family and friends in Twin Peaks were there, all too familiar–yet new. It was a high I would ride on for several years. So much so that when *The Return* was announced in 2014, I fell to the floor in happy tears. Returning to the town of Twin Peaks was everything I'd been waiting and praying for. In retrospect, maybe that was too high of a bar for it to ever live up to. I sometimes wonder if Lynch and Frost were worried about that, so that's why they went in the exact opposite direction. Ultimately, *The Return* was not what I needed it to be and made me reevaluate my relationship to the world of *Twin Peaks*. "You can never go home again" was the message I received from *The Return*, but I have to tell you—the *Missing Pieces* really made me think I could.

John Thorne (author of *The Essential Wrapped in Plastic: Pathways to Twin Peaks*): We all knew about the deleted scenes from *Fire Walk With Me*. (That's what we called them, "the deleted scenes," before they became known as the *Missing Pieces*.) We had read the original script to *Fire Walk With Me* and visualized these scenes in our minds. We had listened to the actors talk about filming them, and their accounts fueled our imaginations. Then, when the scenes finally appeared, assembled as their own unique entity—the *Missing Pieces*—it was revelation and déjà vu all at once, as if someone had recorded our dreams and played them back for us.

Courtenay Stallings (author of *Laura's Ghost: Women Speak About Twin Peaks*): The *Missing Pieces* absolutely blew my mind. In 2014, we, the audience, got more *Twin Peaks*, which I never thought would happen. Not only did we get more *Twin Peaks*, but we got a chance to see the original characters trapped in stasis—their original ages in the original time the film was shot. For those of us who watched *Fire Walk With Me* when it originally aired, it was as if we hadn't aged either. The most striking aspect of the *Missing Pieces*, though, is how it's not simply a series of deleted scenes sloppily edited together. It is a narrative that functions on its own, separately, but linked to *Fire Walk With Me*. For me personally, the "missing pieces" are the clues, those symptoms of Laura Palmer's abuse that

> are so evident to the audience but not to those closest to her. And there are missed opportunities to help Laura. Sheriff Truman tells Andy to stop tailing Jacques Renault, which, if he had followed, would have led him to the cabin the night when Leland/Bob takes Laura to the boxcar of her death. The scene is striking because there is a lingering moment of quiet after the exchange, which seems to suggest something has transpired—the opportunity to save Laura is gone. That scene alone transformed me.

The feelings that the *Missing Pieces* evoked were powerful, and they were achieved with little editing or music added. Lynch is credited as the editor and director of the *Missing Pieces*. The majority of these scenes are master shots. That means there are no cuts in them. A master is shot from a distance, capturing the entire scene, with all the actors running their lines in one take. After filming the master, a director then shoots the close-ups. The editor then pieces the different shots together. So many of the scenes just run as one take. Not sure if there were close-up versions and Lynch just wanted to show the master, but this gives the scenes a realistic feel, as there are very few cuts. The scene with Bobby and Laura in the basement of the Briggs house evokes such desperation for both characters in the one-take version. You can really see the nuances in the performances by Dana Ashbrook and Sheryl Lee. This scene is just under a minute in the film, but the entire, one-take version in the *Missing Pieces* runs three minutes. It adds depth to the conversation and shows Lee and Ashbrook experiencing a wide range of emotions. The two of them are spectacular in this scene, but in the film, at less that half the length, it becomes a forgettable scene.

A quick aside about this scene. In 2021, I was getting my home inspected by my insurance company. The guy noticed my *FWWM* poster and said, "My aunt's house is in that movie. She lives in Fall City." I said, "Let's find it." I pulled up the movie on my computer and went through the film quickly. He said, "That's it!" when we got to the scene with Laura and Bobby on the couch in the basement of the Briggs house. He said, "That isn't a basement. It is a garage. You see that kayak in the back? That's my brother's. They didn't even bother taking it down. They just put the couch there and made it into a basement." I asked him if the

Some of the dialogue is different in the *Missing Pieces* take compared with the final version of this scene in the film. Photo courtesy of New Line Cinema

upstairs scene with Charlotte Stewart and Don Davis was also filmed at his aunt's house, and he said no. I love how *FWWM* follows me wherever I go. Of course, it could be that there are a million pictures of Sheryl Lee, stacks of *Blue Rose* magazines, boxes of books, and *Twin Peaks* art hanging in just about every room in my house.

One of the side effects of using a master shot is that you can't speed up the pacing. That has never been a concern of Lynch's. He famously screamed in a behind-the-scenes moment during the filming of *The Return*, "Who gives a fucking shit how long a scene is." Lynch also didn't add much of a score to the scenes. That is another big connection to *The Return*. The film and the original series, as I have stated, are wall-to-wall music. *The Return* and the *Missing Pieces* are very lightly scored, and the pacing is "later Lynchian." He changed his overall pacing in films between *FWWM* and *Lost Highway*. Frost stated in *Conversations With Mark Frost* that they had started working on the script for *The Return* in 2011, and the *Missing Pieces* was released in 2014. So Lynch worked on these two projects simultaneously. You can feel the changes in Lynch as a filmmaker between 1992 and 2014.

I would never spend time going through each scene; you can pop in the disk and watch them yourselves, and you should. If you watched them in 2014 and haven't watched them since, watch them again today, because they really are fantastic. But there is one scene that I have to highlight. It's the best scene and a perfect microcosm of the *Missing Pieces*. The scene is called "Smash Up" and stars Peggy Lipton and Everett McGill. They sit in Big Ed's pickup truck, parked by the woods. For those of you who love visiting film locations, this is filmed at Olallie State Park, and the car is parked right behind where Lynch filmed the Deer Meadow fist fight scene.

After consuming a few too many beers, Big Ed takes his own Breathalyzer test, confirming he is drunk. They are going to have to sit this one out cuddling in the back of his truck. Norma turns on the radio to find a tune, and an alternate version of "Theme from Twin Peaks Fire Walk With Me" is playing. In this version, a saxophone carries the melody. As the song plays in the dark cab of the truck, these two seasoned actors convey to the audience with only a look how their lives are filled with pain. The song reflects their feelings, and our hearts break. The scene ends with twenty seconds of the music, their faces, the trees, and the darkness. In the pilot, Big Ed and Norma sit at a bar at night as

The scene is an acting lesson from two seasoned pros, but within the story of the film, it had to go. Photo courtesy of New Line Cinema

the theme from the series ("Falling") plays; here, the theme from the film plays for them. Lynch, who picked the music for both scenes, certainly has an affinity for these two characters and feels that their love story is central to *Twin Peaks*. That can be confirmed by his decision to score each of these scenes to the theme of the respective project. In fact, their story is the only original-character arc that is brought to completion in *The Return*. "Smash Up" is a quintessential *Twin Peak*s scene, but cutting it from the film was the exact right thing to do. These two characters are so far outside of the central story that there would have been no justification for including it in the film. Art is about making hard choices to better your story. This was in 1992, and Lynch was still interested in telling stories tied to plot. He was still a highly disciplined filmmaker. So he cut it. (***Comedy trigger warning*** If he had made *FWWM* in 2017, he very well might have included the scene and then cut to someone raking the forest for three minutes.)

While all the scenes were incredible and absolutely invigorating to view after so much time had passed, they also were not relevant to the main story of Laura Palmer and her suffering. The film that Lynch wanted to make was about Laura Palmer. Excising Pete Martell, Big Ed, Sheriff Truman, Lucy, and Andy kept the focus tight on the Palmer family. There have been some clever internet editors who, with the help of the shooting script, have added in the deleted scenes and created a completed version. I will admit I have never watched any of those fan edits. I get the appeal, and I see why fans would do it. But I think it takes away Lynch's most prized possession in his life—final cut. David Lynch told Richard A. Barney in *David Lynch Interviews*: "I would rather not make a film than make one where I don't have final cut." Lynch wanted these deleted scenes to play as a separate film. He looks at the *Missing Pieces* as its own entity. Lynch's overall style changed after *FWWM*. It is so obvious to me, after rewatching all his films in order, that he changed his feelings about pacing somewhere in the early nineties. Compare *Wild at Heart* with *Mulholland Dr.* and you will see. There is a different feel to the editing of the *FWWM* when compared with how he complied the *Missing Pieces*. If Lynch wanted to edit those scenes back into the narrative when releasing them, he could have. They don't belong in the film; they belong alongside it. Yes, it is amazing to see new scenes with

Jack Nance, Don Davis, and Frank Silva, all of whom are no longer with us, but they are in scenes that Lynch felt distracted from the overall story. I love the scene where Pete, Josie, and Dell Mibbler (who is a superminor character in the ABC series) interact about the size of a two-by-four. It is beautifully staged, with the sun and the wood starting the scene off. It is a wonderful study of how life changes with time. But what does that have to do with Laura Palmer? How can that scene compete with her suffering? It had to go.

A side benefit of the *Missing Pieces* is that they offer a gateway into observing how Lynch shapes a scene. Two of the sequences could be used in a class for filmmakers who *think* they want to be the next David Lynch. If you look at the way the Leland Palmer/Teresa Banks scenes play in the film and compare them with the *Missing Pieces*, you will see what he does with editing. The story in the *Missing Pieces* unfolds like any other story in any other movie. Leland calls Teresa, sets up a sexual encounter, then asks her to bring some friends. Leland arrives and sees Laura is one of the girls. Teresa realizes that he knows one of the girls and plans to blackmail him, so he kills her. The deleted scenes spell the story out completely. In the film version, you get only flashes of that story, part of it from Laura's perspective, part from Leland's. I didn't fully comprehend every detail the first time I saw the film, but I did come to understand it the more I watched the film. Look, it's trying to think.

Lynch does the same thing with Phillip Jeffries and the Buenos Aires/FBI scenes. The *Missing Pieces* edit tells the story in order. Viewers can understand it because it is linear. The edits in the film are short, with bursts of static. It's great to understand it, but it's more fun to have to figure it out. It demonstrates to potential filmmakers how a cut can change everything. Yes, it is great, especially in a mystery, not to give too much away, but you have to allow the viewer to not be confused. Questions are good; confusion is bad. We may not be able to grasp every intention, but we have to be able to follow the plot.

The choices Lynch made were not inconsequential, and may be debated for years. For instance, making just a simple cut to a simple establishing shot made all the difference to viewers in Europe, but not in America. Which cut was that? And what effect did it have? Well, go on to the next chapter and find out.

CHAPTER 9

Welcome to Canada?

When you have been a *Twin Peaks* fan for as long as I have, the only fun left to be had is to find something out that you didn't know before. It doesn't happen often. That isn't a statement of ego or hubris; it just is what happens when you waste, I mean, ummm, study something for more than half your life. An example: pretend you know the alphabet. Like you could say all the letters with no trouble. Well, imagine if you found out there was a new letter. One between D and E. You'd be pretty intrigued, wouldn't you? It would give you something new to think about. That is what happened to me on September 24, 2020, while I was playing Twingo online with the Double R Club.

I just realized that I better explain Twingo and the Double R Club first. I would be so happy if by the time this book comes out in 2022, the global pandemic caused by COVID-19 is all but forgotten. In 2020, the world came to a halt because of it, and we all had to stay indoors for about three months in total lockdown and another three months in semilockdown. (Depending on if you believed in science or not. It was a really strange time.) Rose Thorne and Benjamin Louche created and run the Double R Club, a David Lynch-esque cabaret club in London. They decided to play online bingo through their Facebook page, but instead of calling out "B6" or "N25," they called "Agent Cooper" or "This is where we live, Shelly." About fifty *Twin Peaks* fans from around the globe tried to type "Twingo" first to win such prizes as buttons with sayings from the series, owls, or coffee beans. On this particular episode of Twingo, they called "The Power and the Glory." (I didn't have that one, but I did call Twingo that day and won first place for the only time.) If you are not familiar with how "The Power and the Glory" correlates to *Twin Peaks*, then you haven't seen the *Missing Pieces*. In a deleted scene, Laura, Donna, Buck, and Tommy enter The Pink Room, where the topless dancing takes place, from the outside, and there is a sign on the door that says "The Power and the Glory."

It would appear that is the name of the back room of the bar. To make it more confusing, the movie script calls the back room Party Land, and the end credits to *FWWM* list the band's name as The Power & The Glory, but the *Missing Pieces* lists the band as The Pink Room. Here is another great example of how referencing something in the world of *Twin Peaks* is so hard to do correctly. So who knows if The Power and the Glory is a band or a bar? This is why I just call this place The Pink Room.

An establishing shot that was cut ends up creating confusion for fans around the world. Photo courtesy of New Line Cinema

I came up with this name from the title of the song that plays during the beginning of the scene. On the *FWWM* soundtrack, that song is called "The Pink Room." David Lynch movies are never easy to decipher to begin with, but when it comes to names, it gets really confusing. It's about to get worse.

While calling out Twingo clues, Benjamin Louche said, "The bar that they go to, that we all assumed was in the back room at The Roadhouse, which is actually another bar in Canada." Ben was talking about the scene where Laura, Donna, Buck, and Tommy go from The Roadhouse to the seedy bar with all the dance music and nudity.

First of all, I must explain that Ben and Rose are incredibly entertaining, but beneath all their comedy, they truly are *Twin Peaks* scholars. It is incredible how much they know about the series. Writers can't tell jokes, do skits, create poems, and perform cabaret tributes about something unless they know it inside and out. So I couldn't believe it when Ben said "that we all assumed was in the back room at The Roadhouse." Who the heck ever assumed that? I had never once thought the Pink Room sequence was at The Roadhouse. Why would you?

****Comedy trigger warning**** This next paragraph contains jokes about *Twin Peaks.* Only read if you are able to laugh at something you love and are not part of the I-get-offended-easily new trend.

Who thinks that Laura Palmer just goes down to The Roadhouse in the center of a small town and takes her top off and dances around? Then, four days later, when Agent Cooper and Harry Truman go around asking townsfolk if they had seen anything strange with Laura recently, the townsfolk just respond, "Nah, pretty normal. She was here for Tits-'n'-Wings night. Just a typical Tuesday in Twin Peaks." I mean, if you show up on a Wednesday night, are you going to see Doc and Eileen Hayward ripping their clothes off and dancing? Is Monday when Lucy and Andy perform cunnilingus in the back booth? Be sure to watch out for the Log Lady's pitch gum, Mr. and Mrs. Brennan. It's an insane thought. But I really want to see that done as an *SNL* skit. I guess they did say that in a town like Twin Peaks, no one is innocent.

I didn't understand how Ben and Rose could make this mistake. First, when Laura and crew walked into The Pink Room, Laura said, "Welcome to Canada." It is spelled out on the bottom of the screen. Not to mention it is a completely different set. It doesn't feel like The Roadhouse at all. Oh, and what about the fact that the band in this new room is topless? That's a pretty damn big clue you aren't in the local pub where the mayor holds the Miss Twin Peaks tryouts. Julee Cruise never sang "Rockin' Back Inside My Heart" with her butt hanging out. The music, the set, the lighting, and the feel are all very far from The Roadhouse. This new scene is erotic, scary, creepy, and heartbreakingly sad, all at the same time. It couldn't take place in the same town that catapulted this damaged and abused child to the heights of sainthood while ignoring her suffering. She had to escape to a world of debauchery because she felt so bad about herself. She surrounded herself with strangers so that no one could see what she had become. This is exactly why she DOESN'T want Donna to come with her. And why it breaks her when Donna is corrupted by this "other world" that is so far from home, yet so entwined with exactly what happens to Laura when she *is* home.

So why couldn't these brilliant *Twin Peaks* scholars from across the pond see that this was a different bar, in Canada? I needed to know how they made this mistake, so I asked them politely through the Facebook Live comments. OK, I might have been a little snarky. I commented, "No one EVER thought this was at The Roadhouse, because we can all read." Spoken like a true know-it-all. What I didn't know was that Ben and Rose had a completely different viewing experience with *FWWM* than I did because they live in England.

They went on to explain that in Europe, *FWWM* didn't originally have subtitles upon release. Well, fine, but that was a long time ago. What about all the times they'd watched the film since? What about when they saw it on VHS, DVD? I mean, come on, CBS has released *FWWM* more times than The Beatles have released special editions of *Abbey Road*. Well, as it turns out, the theatrical, VHS, and DVD releases never had subtitles in Europe. So the scene in The Pink Room, which includes such classic dialogue as "I'm as blank as a fart" and "I am the muffin," could be understood only if you cranked up the volume and struggled to make out what the characters were saying. In America, "Welcome to Canada" was right there for me to read from the first time I saw the film

Compare the same scene of the American release above with the UK DVD playing on Rose Thorne's TV to the side. No Subtitles.

Even scenes outside The Pink Room are missing the subtitles.

The DVD depicted to the left is just one of the UK releases that didn't have subtitles. This caused viewers outside the United States to miss important dialogue.

Photos courtesy of New Line Cinema and Rose Thorne

in the theater. I was not aware until 2014, when the first Blu-ray set was released, that other countries didn't get subtitles.

At the same time that Europeans finally got a release with subtitles, they got the *Missing Pieces*, which has the deleted scene showing the foursome driving to a new place and entering a bar through a secret door that says "Can-a-do and U S Of Fucking A." There was nothing to be confused about anymore. They also read the line "Welcome to Canada." I remember thinking when I saw the *Missing Pieces* for the first time that there was really no need to see them drive to the next bar, as it was obvious that it was a new place, for the reasons stated above. But maybe deleting that scene was a mistake, because it does seem that it was difficult for viewers to understand that the foursome had relocated to a new venue without it and the accompanying text on-screen. While I would love to judge Rose and Ben for making this mistake, I can't put myself in their new shoes because I always knew where that back room was. Maybe I too would have thought it was strip-down Friday at The Roadhouse. But this led to bigger questions: Why were the subtitles used only in America? And what other scenes in the film didn't have subtitles in Europe?

The Convenience Store scene; the scene with Laura, Mrs. Tremond, and the grandson outside of the Double R Diner; Laura's dream inside the picture; the Pink Room bar scene; Leland's entrance to The Red Room with Bob, OAM, and MFAP—all have subtitles in the American version. Rose, who kept her original DVD, checked all these scenes, and they DO NOT have subtitles. Even if you select the subtitles option, the rest of the film has closed-captioning, but all of the above-mentioned scenes do not.

It would be hard for me to comment on what it would have been like to watch *FWWM* in 1992 without the subtitles on-screen. I never once confused where The Pink Room was. I decided I needed to hear from the masses to see if they were confused about where The Pink Room took place. I asked through *The Blue Rose* Twitter account if people had been confused before the Blu-ray release, which seemed to be uniform in its release.

Here are some of the responses:

@Anton_Binder: Until the *Missing Pieces*, I thought it was a secret room in The Roadhouse or at least another bar in Twin Peaks and "Welcome to Canada" was just some enigmatic dialogue like "I'm the muffin." Also the idea of Twin Peaks being near the Canadian border didn't mean much to us Brits.

@DavidLynchArg: We are from Argentina and never once had it crossed our minds that this scene was in the back of The Roadhouse

@dugpa: Well . . . if memory serves correct, UK theatrical and home entertainment versions didn't have subtitles during the scene which could have led to the mass belief.

@keithgow: If you miss the Canada line or just assume that was a nonsense line like lots of stuff Jacques says in that scene, it's easy to think it's part of The Roadhouse. The script/deleted scenes make it clear.

I posted the same question on my personal Facebook page. I ended up getting eighty-five comments. Eighty-five! To put that in perspective, when I announced that I had conducted the first interview with Alicia Witt about her work for Lynch EVER in her freaking career and that she would be the cover girl of Issue 14, I got none.

Here is a sample of the responses:

Mario Juengling: In Germany, there were no subtitles and I always thought the scene happened at The Roadhouse in the wee hours . . . I did not question it at all. I was too taken away with the sound and the light and the whole sleazy scenario. Honestly, it arouses me everytime I watch it! It is the perfect part of *FWMM*. The *Missing Pieces* made it clear for me though that it happened across the border.

Cheryl Lee Latter: I think because Jacques was there too, and we had just seen him working, I thought it was an invite-only sleazy back room.

Dave Arambarri-Somers: Jacques Renault would have

had some shit to deal with at the bar or something if it was his place.

(I love this comment from Dave. This is so *Twin Peaks* to me. Do you see how logical that is? Think of all the strangeness that Lynch is known for. Dave is 100 percent correct. If this was The Roadhouse, Jaques would be working. Fans of the show believe in this world. They live in it. They believe in these characters like it is, like it sounds. ****Comedy trigger warning**** I love the idea that Jacques would be working the bar while simultaneously dropping pills in beers and making out with Ronette Pulaski. Jacques is waiting on Major and Betty Briggs, who are waiting for their cheese fries and second round of Diet Cokes at The Roadhouse. They can't find their waiter because he is in the back room going down on some rando. I just really struggle to think that people thought this nude fest was at The Roadhouse.)

Eric Billingsley: It's the anti-Roadhouse . . . Just like Deer Meadow is the anti-Twin Peaks.

(Another reason why I think it is called The Pink Room: because it is on the road to The Red Room.)

Sammy Catto: I never thought it was The Roadhouse. Very clearly somewhere different. Just by who's there and how they're behaving.

Maja Ljunggren: I saw it in a cinema in Sweden with very loud sound, and it was not subtitled, and I loved it that way, because it was just as if you were there, at a loud bar and you have no idea what your friends are saying. I agree with you, Scott. I never thought it was at The Roadhouse. I grew up in a town very much like Twin Peaks, and you could never have gotten away with getting naked in a bar in your hometown without the whole town knowing it within seconds. (Yes, even in a secret room.) So if you wanted to do stuff, you had to drive at least an hour away if you didn't want everybody to find out. So I assumed they were far away from home. And that makes the whole thing even scarier. Laura takes drugs, Donna gets drugged and if Laura wouldn't have stopped it, Donna could have ended up in a ditch somewhere far away and nobody would have known. Now they are dependent on someone driving them back to Twin Peaks.

Bruce Green: It's interesting to me that Scott says "maybe the movie didn't have subtitles in England when it played in theaters." It didn't have subtitles in the USA either, at least not when I saw it at Piper's Alley (Chicago) in 1992. I had the same experience Maja described earlier in this thread, "It was just as if you were there, at a loud bar and you have no idea what your friends are saying." I thought it was an amazing Lynchian touch; we followed along like a silent movie. Did other people in the USA see subtitles on the original viewing?

Anita K. Dunning-Rehn: Bruce, nope, no subtitles when I saw it in the theatre the first time. I actually prefer it without subtitles. Like you said, I think for me, it takes me out of

The left side is The Roadhouse, the right side is The Pink Room. Do they look the same to you? Photos courtesy of CBS and New Line Cinema

the experience. I think you put it perfectly that it is as if you were in the bar with them and not completely being able to hear exactly what they are saying. You have to concentrate harder on what's going on, which is extremely hard for me in this scene. When I saw this in the theater for the first time it was incredibly disturbing for me.

Jason Sheppard: I can attest these subtitles were on the Canadian VHS and DVD versions of *FWWM*.

Aaron Cohen: I can confidently say that for many years I thought this scene happened just underneath where they were before. I pictured some secret stairs down to this seedy extra room. I think I also thought the "Welcome to Canada" line was a throwaway just like "blank as a fart." As in "you're partying with some cool Canadians now, welcome to Canada!"

Lindsay Hallam: In Australia the scene had subtitles so I always thought it was a different location and not The Roadhouse. I also bought a copy of the shooting script which makes it clearer they went somewhere else.

Brad Payne: It definitely had subtitles when I saw it (twice) in Michigan on opening day. I've actually never heard of an instance before now where a print shown during the original U.S. run didn't have subtitles.

Bruce Green: Well, I can't say what anyone else saw, but what I saw in Chicago 1992 did not have the subtitles. This is a no-doubter for me; the inaudible dialogue was one of the things my *Twin Peaks* friends and I discussed extensively immediately after viewing. That, and what the hell did the monkey say?

Faye Murman: I truly thought this was the back of The Roadhouse until I got a little older and figured it out on a rewatch in college.

Rob Perino: Same. I went years without considering or realizing "Canada" literally meant Canada. "Canada" is the only indicator of location change, because there is no clear visual transition.

Cheryl Lee Latter: I have to agree with them! I watched the film dozens of times before the *Missing Pieces*, and I honestly never knew they went to a second location until then. It was genuinely impossible to hear anything they said in the original UK version, and my VHS had no subtitles.

So why did I make you read my Facebook page? Good question. There isn't a better example of the *Twin Peaks* community than these comments and posts. When the pandemic started, I arranged a three-hour live event with over ten *Twin Peaks* actors for free; I got maybe five comments about the end result. But ask about a plot point like where the bar was AND challenge what they saw, felt, or thought about a scene from *Twin Peaks* and you get eighty-five comments. (While I was writing this very sentence my post got two more comments.) This wasn't posted through *The Blue Rose* Facebook page. This all happened on my personal page. I do leave my page open to the public, so anyone can comment, but still, that is a ton of responses to a simple question. It sparked debate and gave fans a chance to say that they were there in 1992. Whether the few American commenters really didn't have subtitles or if they remember it incorrectly, who knows? Maybe the projectionist cut the bottom of the screen off? Maybe they were there? Maybe a few European prints slipped through? Questions in a world of blue, my friends.

Here is what I do know: everyone has an opinion about where Laura and Donna boogied. But in a larger sense, it is an unintentional example of how important editing is. Hard choices had to be made to whittle the film down to a releasable length. Cutting the car ride and entrance to the new bar made an impact, as did the error of the subtitles not making it to the final film in Europe. But it also shows that an audience can fill in the blanks when given a chance. I guess that in the end, after seeing that scene for thirty years and never doubting where it took place, I will now always think whenever I watch it: "Huh, some people thought the townsfolk of Twin Peaks got naked at The Roadhouse? Are you kidding me?"

CHAPTER 10

The M.O. of Mary Sweeney

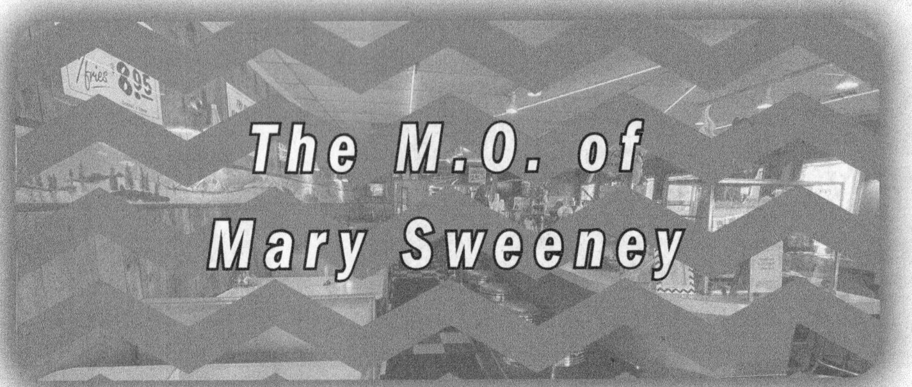

Mary Sweeney had a hand in so many amazing Lynch film moments. She edited *Lost Highway*, *The Straight Story*, *Mulholland Dr.*, and *FWWM*. She was a producer on several of those as well as the screenwriter of *The Straight Story*. She also edited Episode 14, one of the most famous episodes of *Twin Peaks*'s original run, which revealed the killer of Laura Palmer, plus the pilot episodes of *On the Air* and *Hotel Room*, so she is royalty for a Lynchian like myself. For years I have wanted to interview her about her stellar career. I could have spent hours on each of the above projects, but this book is about *FWWM*, so I tried to stay there. I found her to be intelligent and insightful, and I loved that she had absolutely no problem disagreeing with me. That is what I look for in any discussion I get into. I am a proud member of Gen X; we were raised to debate and discuss with our loved ones. Mary Sweeney, who now is a professor at the University of Southern California, was more than willing to disagree, always with the intention of getting it right. And she has gotten so many film moments exactly right.

Scott Ryan: We're going to get to *FWWM* questions, but I watched *Lost Highway* again yesterday; I hadn't seen it in a while. And it made me wonder if as an editor, do you have to understand what a movie is about to edit it?

Mary Sweeney: That's a very amorphous question. First of all, I have a script. So I know what the movie is about, and David shoots the script—even when on the page it says Bill Pullman freaks out and wakes up as Balthazar Getty. With David, you are the spectator now. People who do or don't like David's movies walk into a movie theater for a new David Lynch movie leaving their expectations at the door. You are assuming that you will not *exactly* know what's going on. That sort of describes a little bit how I would approach reading a new script by David.

When I cut initially, I'm just following the script and David's preferences. I do my best to give him the fattest, fullest, ugliest assembly, so that he feels like I haven't taken liberties, I haven't made critical decisions. That comes much later for me in the process. He trusts me. I think he trusted me more. It was pretty hard to watch him watch that cut. [Laughs.] You kind of wanna kill yourself, because it's so, so bad. But he's a professional; he knows that. I *hope* he understood, though he never articulated it, that I was giving him his full master shots, and I cut in where he wanted me to cut in. I always used his preferred takes, even if they weren't working as well. That way we started with what he came in from the shoot thinking was going to work. Back then, it was a very delicious process—with plenty of time that they don't give people anymore—to look at it, take notes, and me going back and making the changes. We would do that for two or three months, just the two of us, not anybody else seeing it.

Ryan: And that's on *FWWM* or *Lost Highway*?

Sweeney: That's on everything we did together.

Ryan: When was the beginning of *FWWM* for you?

Sweeney: When we went up to the Seattle area to start shooting, which was I think August or September of '91.

Ryan: Did you think, "I like this idea of going backward and telling Laura Palmer's story?" As a fan, how did you feel about that?

Sweeney: Well, I am a fan, of course. It's a funny way to think about it. It was such an incredible stroke of luck for me to be hired by Duwayne Dunham on *Blue Velvet* as his editing assistant in the San Francisco Bay Area. I mean, all of the circumstances leading up to that happening, and my starting to work with David, are just so complicated, as life is—that I was living in the Bay Area, that Duwayne's regular assistant took the big George Lucas job as his assistant. And I got *Blue Velvet*—a $3 million, kind of strange film.

I knew about *Eraserhead*, of course, and I also loved *Elephant Man*. But I just love David's kind of filmmaking, and it was so incredible that I fell into exactly the kind of films that I loved. At the time that I was moving from the second season of *Twin Peaks* to do *FWWM*, that was a huge leap for me. I was going from being a swing editor on the series to a lead editor on the film. When someone's cutting film—unless you're working with an editor who gives you scenes or is mentoring you in that way—you have no way of actually getting experience cutting film. It's kind of crazy how impossible it was to have access to literally cutting two shots together—forget about scenes. So many people had lifelong careers as assistant editors, picture editors in film, because especially in Hollywood studios, it was a good union job. You could support a family. And it's just really hard to move from assisting into editing.

So that's what was on my mind: I was going to be cutting this film by myself. I was completely excited. There was no judgment involved. It was such an incredible and exciting opportunity for me to work with him. I'd had a taste of it while editing Episode 14 of *Twin Peaks*. I would say—I can't really speak for him—that it was a good partnership. It was a very good creative partnership. I understood things emotionally. He had to say very little to me to get the feeling that he wanted to get.

Ryan: So you cut the episode where viewers found out who killed Laura Palmer?

Sweeney edited Episode 14 with Lynch. That was their first project together.
Photo courtesy of CBS

Sweeney: Yes, it was a challenge, especially that last scene, in The Roadhouse while the murder is going on. The inner cutting between those two—that was a stew where we just, right out of the gate, really clicked. It was both really heartbreaking, on one side in The Roadhouse, and horrifying, in the Palmer house.

Ryan: Oh, yeah, I mean, congratulations on cutting that. That is the most classic scene in all of *Twin Peaks*, really.

Sweeney: Thank you.

Ryan: That's incredible. I'm assuming you were there for the filming of *FWWM*?

Sweeney: Yes, I was.

Ryan: I believe that Sheryl Lee's performance in *FWWM* is the greatest female performance captured on film. I don't care if I'm not allowed to pick the greatest, I just think it's incredible what she did. What was that like to witness that?

Sweeney: It was an amazing performance. But there are so many different kinds of films and performances, so it's hard to say "the greatest" about anything.

Ryan: Well, you don't have to say it was the greatest. But I think it is.

Sweeney: I know, and I'm neither denying nor confirming. I'm just saying it's such a hard job for actors and actresses. She was phenomenal, to get to your question. She was amazing. First of all, I'm never on set when I am editing—I'm always trying to keep up to camera. Everything I get, I look at the dailies and start cutting right away so I'm not too far behind when they wrap, so it won't take me too long to have an assembly for David. We were all staying in this hotel, the Red Lion. And you could just see that it was taking all of Sheryl's strength to play that role day after

Sheryl Lee gives it her all in every scene of the film. Photo courtesy of New Line Cinema

day. It was so impressive. She was so professional, so serious, so incredibly communicative in all the stuff going on inside, all the dark stuff and all of the daylight stuff of Laura. It's just a very complex role. She was in so much of the film. The first cut was very long, like five and a half hours, because we had all these characters from the series. It was a staggering job for her to undertake, and her performance was unbelievable.

I would see it on film; I wouldn't see it while it was being shot. That was already pretty staggering, the intensity of her performance and the scenes. But when the film gets to me, it's like solving a puzzle. And just that kind of focus mediates what you're actually looking at—what she's actually going through. When I first began cutting, it's just trying to put it together in the first assembly in the way that I can tell from the notes and the way David wrote the script and the way he shot the scenes what he's going into the scene thinking he wants. After he sees that and we take notes, then I make changes, and we keep doing that. Then it starts to be, for me, more about making myself—if I can—feel the emotion that you want the audience to feel in a particular scene—whatever the emotional content is. It's both sides of my brain at work, where I'm thinking about the logic of the scene and also the music of it—like how it flows—and inside the music part of it is where the emotional content needs to connect for me.

Ryan: Do you think the fact that you were a female editor helped shape Sheryl Lee's performance and what she goes through?

Sweeney: The general part of the question, I don't know what I can say about male, female, as editors, but specifically, somehow I did connect with David on the very emotional side of his work. You see it very clearly in *Elephant Man*, for example. And I think in *The Straight Story* too. But it's there, and in his most difficult films. *Lost Highway* is a really difficult film, but I think that the mixture of tenderness and, as he's so fond of saying, "darkness and confusion" is just something that I understood. You never know why people meet in certain ways—it's so random. We're all so different from each other. So I don't know that it was my being a woman as much as it was my being someone who considers myself an artist and is interested in the full range of human emotions. Using what he shot, what he wrote, and how he directed, those are the tools in editing. They were just such a gift to any editor. I just dove in.

Ryan: You said that you had to learn how to cut two things together, and sometimes, if you're a novice at something, you don't know how hard something is going to be because you haven't done it before. Do you look back now and think, "Holy crap, I had to edit *FWWM* with no experience?" Do you think it helped that you were a novice?

Sweeney: No, you know, I had no hesitation like that. I wasn't afraid of it. I was very excited for the opportunity to jump in and cut it by myself. But I'd also been functioning as a swing editor on the TV series, and that was very hard for me, to transition from assisting to cutting. There were three full-time editors on Season 2. We were all cutting in film, and they would give me scenes. It was like a little tutorial; I got scenes from three different editors. They'd give me notes, and then I'd bring it back again. So it was exactly the kind of training or opportunity that a lot of people don't get. When I cut Episode 14, I cut that whole thing, which had a lot of complicated stuff.

By that point, it was me cutting it, but David would come in, and we'd go through it, and he'd give me his notes. I couldn't have had a better tutorial. I was foot on the block, champing at the bit to cut a film. So I was definitely not long on cutting feature films in experience, but I felt totally ready. It was very stressful, because I had a crew of my own and we had major deadlines to meet. Then we went to Cannes, all that kind of stuff. But editing is very stressful, especially back in the days of film. Incredibly stressful!

Ryan: One of the scenes I love in *FWWM* is where Donna and Laura are talking on the couches and the camera starts way up high and then it doesn't really move forward, but you keep cutting closer to Laura's face. I always analyzed this scene as the camera doesn't get that close to Donna because she's safe. But Laura is not safe. And by the end scene, when Laura's talking about The Angel and bursting into flames, the camera is so close it's just her eyes. Nothing is going to escape it. When you are editing a scene like that, are you saying, "Let's keep cutting close to her," and you give that to David? How does a scene like that come to be?

Sweeney: It's hard to remember stuff because I do get so invested in making it work, which is part logic and part the mystery of what cuts work and part immersing myself in what's going on in this scene emotionally. So, for example, that's a combination of things. David wasn't in the room when I'd start a scene, but he also wouldn't sit down and say, "I want to move in just on Laura here." All that kind of stuff you just said—your interpretation—he never talked that way; he never communicated any kind of "This is what I'm trying to do here." He doesn't do that with any of us. Not with Angelo Badalamenti, not with Peter Deming [DP on *Lost Highway*]. You have to be on David's wavelength, because you might be kind of freaked out otherwise.

I get the dailies. I see the script. I see what he shot. I see that he's going in super close. My recollection isn't necessarily that he only went super close on Laura, but my guess would be probably he didn't shoot quite as much of that stuff on Donna. So I sort of follow what I'm reading of his intention and from the script. Another example of that is the Club Silencio scene with Rebekah Del Rio in *Mulholland Dr.* [See photo below, courtesy of Universal.]

When the intensity of the emotion is meant to be building, I get the sense—and so do many other filmmakers throughout history—to cut in

closer on the actor. In that case, just before she collapses, where it's the full-on giant close-up of Rebekah belting out that song, and then cutting to the girls, who were increasingly emotional, it's like just a conversation between the two of them, and you're kind of caught inside it. But that's an emotion, and to get that emotion you kind of just have to work and work until it's all lined up the way it needs to be, to be that musical flow. Not the song she's singing, but the music of the scene. The emotional music of the scene.

Ryan: I love this interview! I love your answers, and this is something I've waited thirty years for, and I'm just having the time of my life. I think I'm not supposed to tell you that, so pretend I just went right on with this: you had mentioned that *FWWM* was a five-hour movie, and you've got to get it down to two hours and fifteen minutes. I am so fascinated by this as just a piece of art. Basically what happens is that all of Lynch's friends get cut. Charlotte Stewart? Sorry. You're out. Jack Nance? Hey, you've been in every movie; you're not in this one! What was that experience like? What do you remember about cutting down a five-hour film, and how did you possibly make those decisions?

Sweeney: I think it was five and a half, actually. First of all, just having David accept what the final running time would be if we just trim it down. We would have been lucky to get it down to a three-and-a-half-hour cut. There were so many characters from the TV series, and I think without articulating it, he—as painful as it was—just understood that the things that would have to go were the things that brought characters back but didn't really have to do with this story about Laura Palmer. I don't know when that realization hit. It may have hit him while he was shooting it; I have no idea. Life goes on in his head. So the first thing that happened was that we just excised scenes. We made a path, and said, "This whole scene has to go."

So, a lot of the *Missing Pieces*, I looked at them after that rough assembly, and there were no fine cuts or even medium cuts on those things, and certainly no sound mix on them. But removing entire scenes, that was the simple part of it. Then the final running time was still pretty long, and that was the hard part of it. As much as it broke his heart to cut out those scenes you just mentioned, he's a very responsible filmmaker. He always keeps to the budget and schedule, and I think he just understood that he couldn't keep all those peripheral scenes that had more to do with the series than with the film he was making. I think part of the reception of that film had to do with everybody just wanting to go back into *Twin Peaks* land, and this was a David Lynch movie. It was a different animal.

Ryan: Was there anything that broke your heart to cut?

Sweeney: I mean, generally, I'm sure there were. I can't answer specifically, but there's sometimes scenes you love but you move them around, you try different things, and they just can't live in the film for some reason. You don't really understand it, and that's the kind of thing that David and I were really also in sync with, where I would try and work on something, change it, move it around, and try it here, split it, all different things, and usually we would often get to a point where we'd say, "OK, it's not going to work, we tried all this stuff, we gotta take it out." So it's always hard, and it always requires a lot of work to adjust to make sure it didn't work. This is why David refused for a long time to have DVD chapter breaks. It's like, "No, this is a single piece." The amount of work that's gone into creating this—every frame of this, every sound, every piece of music at these levels—is like a painting: you can't touch it. You can't cut a painting into four sections and let people look at one piece at a time.

Ryan: That's a great statement. I like that. I have said for many years that the only reliable narrator in *FWWM* is the sound. That's where you can really get the story from. Whenever there's something going on with MFAP, the whooping comes in. What is your role in sound as an editor?

Sweeney: Very minimal. Certainly at the stage when I was editing in film. Because David's *very proprietary* [laughs] about sound. He's just so fantastic at it; he loves it so much. When you're cutting in film, at our budget level, you have to do these funny little temp dubs. We worked at Raleigh Studios. They used to have this goofball setup where they'd have three cams and only the center cam had a picture, and the other two were just sound. So you could put up five mag tracks and there was a little mixing thing on the cam, so you could mix four tracks down to one. We did a lot of screening for that kind of really crappy sound before I'd lock the picture and turn it over to sound. Once I've locked the picture, David does so much magic working with the sound crew and working in the mix. He's just a master at sound. *Lost Highway* was the last picture I cut on film, and *The Straight Story* was the first I cut on Avid, although we had done commercials together on Avid. Working on the Avid, I would take the liberty of putting in sound, and he was so sharp, the second that the sound that I put in would play, no matter how subtle I'd do it, he'd give me this look like, "Where did that come from?" and "Take it out now." [Laughs.] Once I was in Avid, I was mixing sound just to clean it up a bit. I didn't cut scenes to music, but there were obviously music scenes like "Llorando," the Rebekah Del Rio song from *Mulholland Dr.*, where it was playback, I had to cut with music. David and Angelo would manipulate the music, of course, too, with an effect—slow it down, double it up, run it backward—so the creativity that happened in the sound mix was David.

Ryan: In the Pink Room scene, in the American release, there are subtitles. Well, in Europe, the movie was released without subtitles. Do you know why?

Sweeney: You're talking about the scene where it's super loud and you can't hear anything, and Jacques says something about a fart?

Ryan: Yeah, he says, "I'm as blank as a fart."

Sweeney: So we definitely subtitled that. There were always subtitles. Oh my God, I laughed so hard when David said we were going to subtitle it. I just thought that was such a fantastic idea. And everytime I see that movie, which is not lately, but I've seen it a lot, it seems really funny to me. Especially what Jacques is saying. But you're telling me that outside of the US, there are no subtitles?

Ryan: It was theatrically released on film with no subtitles. The first time it came out on VHS and DVD, no subtitles. David is so protective of his work, the fact that this would slip through is surprising. I contacted Sabrina Sutherland and asked her about it.

Sweeney: She wouldn't know, because that's a foreign distribution deal. Whether it's dubbed or subtitled is part of the thing, but if we had subtitles they would translate them from the subtitles in English to the subtitles in whatever the local language is. So I can't answer that question for you.

Ryan: There's no way it's intentional. Why would he say, "I only want Americans to understand the dialogue"?

Sweeney: I have no idea. To my recollection, he never said anything like that.

Ryan: Don't you really put the text on the film? It's not like I can take those subtitles off when I watch it. So it's weird that somebody took them off.

Sweeney: Here's what's weird, though: we did subtitle the film when we went to Cannes. I supervised it because I speak French. We had to go over to France a week early so I could work with the subtitler. So we subtitled the film that was presented at Cannes, and I'm sure the subtitles were there. I mean, I wonder if David's got this information. He supervised the *Entire Mystery Box* and said, "Hey, where's the subtitles?" and nobody said, "Oh, we never used them." I wouldn't want to bring that up, either. I wouldn't want to be that person.

Ryan: No, I think he would be very angry to find this out.

Sweeney: He would be *very* angry. There's nothing you can do about it. It's history now. But I think that would be very upsetting, I just want to warn you, that would be extremely upsetting to David if he learned that and wasn't aware of it.

Ryan: The reason it matters is because all of my friends in England thought that that scene happened in the back of The Roadhouse. Because they just didn't get that it was Canada, because they couldn't hear it.

Sweeney: Well, that's unfortunate, honestly. I would maybe just let that rest. Seriously, it's upsetting to me as the editor to hear that—that all these territories didn't see the right film is kind of hard to believe. I don't want David to hear that, honestly.

Lynch, Anderson, and Sweeney at the 1992 Cannes Film Festival
Photo courtesy of New Line Cinema

Ryan: Well, the chances of him reading this book are pretty slim. I'm about to ruin the first line of my book, but you were there so I gotta ask, was *FWWM* really booed at Cannes?

Sweeney: Well, the active booing happens usually at the press screening, which is not the big gala event. David and I were not at the press screening. But we heard that there was booing. Now, was there booing? It was pretty quiet, and this was a long time ago. My recollection of the premiere is that it was in an incredibly beautiful two thousand-seat theater at the Cannes Film Festival, which was one of the most amazing experiences. The screening was very quiet, and then David did press, and it was clear the reception wasn't great. I don't know if we knew when we went into the screening that the film had been booed that morning by the press. We stayed because we had to do press. Then we went back to Paris. It was a strange experience. He had been there two years earlier with *Wild at Heart* and won the Palme d'Or. There were people who were telling us, "Don't go back, it's too soon, you just won." But it's where you want to release your film, and they invited him, so he wanted to go.

I was eight months and two and a half weeks pregnant when we were in Cannes and we had the Cannes experience. He could tell from the press that it was not well received. We didn't talk about it, but for me it was in the context that people wanted the quirky kind of fun and scary *Twin Peaks* TV series. They wanted all their favorite characters. This was a very challenging David Lynch movie, very violent, and he had gotten criticism two years earlier with *Wild at Heart* for being too violent. But it's hard to imagine *that* festival was disturbed by *FWWM* considering what's been screened there since. But it was kind of violent for the time.

It was so mixed. We went back to Paris, and two days later our son was born. So it was personally very fantastic to be there. David's very protective of his work. That's why he insists on final cut. This film was very powerful and kind of tough at times. But I think it was more the expectation that wasn't met that accounts for the reaction. It's tough, but you have to take the bad reviews with the good reviews. That's part of making films. And he always said, "If you don't have final cut, and you have to make compromises or people change your movie, I don't know how you can look at yourself in the mirror." And he said, "This is the way I have to work, and I can take whatever comes." And he did. He never lost faith in himself, and he did not lose faith in the film.

Ryan: What about you? It was your first film. That's easy for him to say; he had made other films. How did you take the negative criticism? Not just at Cannes, but overall. You had to take it personally.

Sweeney: I didn't take it personally, I mean, there were so many people that were very invested in that film, and we loved the film, and it just didn't hit the mark. After the screening, the few days that we were there—you have to be professional no matter what happens. You have to do the press, and you have to be proud of the film and of your work and just put one foot in front of the other. It was a couple of days that we were sort of in the face of it that way. And also, there was so much respect for David. They didn't like that film, but they really love David in France, and you could feel that underneath. I can't explain not feeling devastated. Maybe it was just kind of the third-trimester hormonal bliss you're in [laughs], I don't know. I was very disappointed, but David is so focused on what he does. I didn't worry about him; we just presented the film and went to Paris and had a kid.

Ryan: I love that. I love that you had a kid right then. You probably hear this a lot, but I really did love it the first time I saw it. I think the world was not ready for that story in 1992. They're probably not ready for it today, but at least people accept it more. So it's a beautiful work of art.

Sweeney: There was a huge amount of passion and creativity on David's part that went into that film and the Laura Palmer role in Sheryl Lee's performance. I mean, it's not the kind of thing that—if people boo it—you just kind of flip the switch on and then not care about something that you've been passionate about for a year. You're right where you were the day you stepped off the plane in France. Which is that you're full of hope, and some of your hope is dashed, for sure, but your films are your children. It's not like you're going to divorce them if people don't like the films. It's like, "Well, I don't understand it, because I really love it" kind of feeling. I think *Lost Highway* is another example of what you just said. When I show *Lost Highway* in a class that I teach at USC, nonlinear things do not bother students now. So the fact that the character changes from Bill Pullman to Balthazar Getty and it becomes a different movie just doesn't phase audiences now. He was just ahead of the curve. It was a brilliant idea. And he was challenged a lot on that plot at the time.

David is an avant-garde filmmaker, meaning literally he is leading. He is out in the lead. He's forging a trail.

CHAPTER 11

The One That Is Meant to Help

"I'm so afraid that no one will believe me until after I have taken the seat that I fear has been saved for me in the darkness."—Laura Palmer's final entry in *The Secret Diary of Laura Palmer*, Jennifer Lynch (1990)

I am not one of those writers who believe that location inspires writing, at least for me. This is my sixth book. Writing is my job now. I don't need to set the mood. I can write anywhere, anytime that life allows it. But can I explain to you where I am writing this very sentence? I am sitting on a balcony at the Salish Lodge & Spa, listening to "The Laura Palmer Theme" as the sounds of the Snoqualmie Falls churn in the background. The Douglas firs, which are less than ten feet off my balcony, are blowing in the summer wind. I am wearing a Salish robe while staying at the resort that was the outdoor shooting location for The Great Northern hotel. It was six years ago that I first trekked to Snoqualmie, Washington, to see the sights and feel the mood of where the pilot of *Twin Peaks* and *FWWM* were filmed. That time I came as an attendee of the now-defunct *Twin Peaks* fan festival. Today I am here as a tourist, although with this being my sixth time in the area, it feels more like a homecoming. I am struck by how much my life has changed in those six years.

It took me twenty-five years to finally make the trip out here, and it changed my life. Attending the twenty-fifth Twin Peaks Festival is what started me on this path of publishing *Twin Peaks*-based books and magazines. On that weekend I met for the first time Brad Dukes, who wrote *Reflections: An Oral History of Twin Peaks*; David Bushman, who wrote *Conversations With Mark Frost* and now runs Fayetteville Mafia Press with me; Courtenay Stallings, who wrote *Laura's Ghost* and is one of *The Blue Rose*'s managing editors; Pieter Dom, who runs the *Welcome to Twin Peaks* website; and John Thorne, who did *Wrapped in Plastic*. In addition to meeting these artists, I was introduced to so many people who have become a part of my daily life. All of these connections and all of these artists came into my life and inspired and supported me in a way that I had never been before. But it wasn't just fans whom I met; it was stars from the series as well.

I met Charlotte Stewart (Betty Briggs, plus Mary X in *Eraserhead*) that weekend, and now we are dear friends. I met Catherine Coulson (The Log Lady) while I was browsing in the Salish gift shop, years before I would be brave enough to book a room there. It was there that *she* asked *me* to take a picture of her holding a stuffed log that was on sale so that she could send it to her kids to show them she had done something with her life. I remember immediately saying, "You are The Log Lady. You did more than *something* with your life." I mistakenly brushed it off, thinking about how my kids don't care about what I do either. I didn't think about it very much, because why would I? I was too busy freaking out that I was meeting a legend. She was extra kind to me, as this wasn't at an event. She was just a shopper, like me. She was the first *Twin Peaks* actor I ever met in real life. She had a human conversation with me, treated me as an equal, and I was elated.

For those of you who know me in person or from my online persona, it might come as a shock to you that I battle chronic depression. I have spent the majority of my life putting on a happy face and entertaining strangers because of my inability to experience joy for myself. This was the part I left out when I wrote the introduction, where I shared my remembrance of my first viewing of *FWWM*. When the film premiered in August 1992, I was preparing to graduate from college four months

later. I was surrounded by people who were so excited to be graduating and starting their lives, but not me. I was not majoring in writing or anything creative. I was majoring in marketing because I was too scared to tell the people who surrounded me that I wanted to do something creative with my life, not something safe, and by no means did I want to do something boring. My greatest fear was that I would end up in a tiny cubicle selling something that had no meaning or purpose. You know, the very place my complacent ass sat when I heard the devastating news that Catherine Coulson was dead—only six weeks after our brief encounter at the Salish.

I have talked many times about how that chance meeting and then her shocking death—shocking to me at least, because I had no idea she was battling cancer when she was asking me to take a picture for her children—rocked me out of my complacency. I was working in a cubicle at a global communications company, spending my days not using my talents as a writer. This had been my crime for nearly forty years. I looked around the soulless corporation, listening to pointless phones ringing with problems and complaints that never would be addressed. I stood up, my head poking above the fake walls, and looked for an answer. It wasn't gonna be found there, not for me. I had to change or I wasn't gonna make it. I kept thinking, What if I died in six weeks? Would I be pleased with how I had wasted my life never trying? I was immediately knocked back to my first viewing of *FWWM* and the despair I was experiencing at that point in my life, as I sat in the darkened theater. All those years later, sitting in my corporate cubicle under the six-foot-long fluorescent bulbs that brightened the office but not my soul, I felt gripped by the same paralyzing despair.

What I saw in Laura Palmer was someone who was pretending for everyone else's benefit. Someone hiding a secret she couldn't tell. Part of the reason I have never spoken about this is because I know how much worse all the women who have been sexually abused and looked to Laura for hope had it. It wasn't that my secret compared to theirs, but seeing Laura in *FWWM* was the first time I saw someone put on a social, happy face while dying inside. The way the town saw Laura, despite her being lost, was how I felt everyone viewed me. When someone is forced into a world where they don't want to be, to be someone other than who they really are, and to suppress it for the good of the people who are supposed to be there to support them—that is a horrible place to be, no matter the circumstances.

Sheryl Lee's unrestrained performance gave me the strength to keep going. A movie in which the "happy ending" is that the main character dies? Now you were talking my lingo. As for my personal struggle, however, there seemed to be no happy ending in sight. I didn't expect to be visited by an angel or to bathe in the glow of an otherworldly blue light. I had no hope. I was certain that my life would follow the safe path, that I'd make no attempt to break free of it. From 1992 to 1997, I created no art. I didn't write a word. If you look at all I have done since 2017, you will then understand how unnatural that was for me. I created nothing, but I watched *FWWM* over and over again. I didn't understand why at the time. It took me years to realize how I had latched onto Laura's strength to get me through those years and those that followed. The film empowered me to continue on for twenty-five years with no hope. Whenever I was lost and feeling that there was no point in living, and it happened often, or when my very existence seemed pointless, I watched Laura. Or, more specifically, Sheryl Lee. I knew Laura wasn't real. But Sheryl was doing something in that performance that I had never seen before. She became an avatar for my pain, my duality. She didn't leave a safe space between the audience and her performance. She laughed harder than she should have out in the woods with Dana Ashbrook. She cried harder than she should have under the bush outside of the Palmer house. She bared her soul and her body not in a sexual way, but in a raw, painful, fearless way that just wasn't normally captured on film. I wish I was brave enough to do more of that here, but I am no Sheryl Lee. I never wanted to meet Laura Palmer. For me, it was Sheryl the artist whom I watched. She delivered a true reflection of how pointless depression feels. We all knew Laura was going to die; there was nothing to be done about it. It was written in the stars. There was no way out. And for those years, "no way out" was all I knew.

In 2015, Catherine was my angel. Without knowing it, she saved me by making me see how short life is. It was offensive to her memory for me to squander another moment of it. Three years later, I sat across from Sheryl Lee, and I thanked her for saving my life. For keeping me alive until circumstances allowed me to become who I was supposed to be. To share my art and write about what I wanted to. I have peers who inspire me to be better and accept me for who I am. I do not have to sell my soul to a corporation just so that an executive can buy a third boat. I found a partner in my wife, who supports me and gives me the courage to step out into the world. Jen is my angel.

So now I sit at the Salish and write this missing piece of my story for the first time. I do it with the hope that if you are out there and not where you should be in life, let me shine a light of change on you. I have lived on both sides. I have done what was asked of me, and I have done what I was born to do. To be honest, no one else really cared which path I traveled. The only person it truly affected was me. So be yourself. Any success I have had was because I moved forward and became the person I truly am. If you are struggling today, I can't give you any better advice than to hear the voice of love and be who you are, not who people want you to be. It took me almost thirty years, but I got out of that darkened theater and found enough light to survive. The proof is that today I texted Sheryl Lee and asked her when she wanted to do the interview for this book. There is no way twenty-two-year-old Scott would have believed, or even have been able to conceive of the possibility, that he would get to live this life, where Sheryl would know his name. Becoming friends with Sheryl was set in motion because Catherine said to me, "I want my kids to know I did something." Within a month of Catherine's passing, I started *The Blue Rose* magazine. Trust me, no one was further away from realizing their potential, their dream, or shedding their baggage than that punk college kid who watched *FWWM* and feared that his life was just shown on the big screen. I wasn't gonna meet The Log Lady or Laura Palmer, or be surrounded with friends who were artists. For so many years, I believed my only option was to end up in the train car. To take the ring. But even though it took me decades, I became who I was always born to be. It happened through hard work, dedication, and never giving up. Laura got one angel; I got several. I've dedicated this book to Jen, Lisa, Courtenay, Janet, Sheryl, and Catherine. I have been lucky to be saved by so many wonderful women who have opened me up to the world.

I walked down to the falls and listened to "Falling" as I spied the same view that the television cameras captured in the opening credits. It looked exactly like what I had first seen on my television screen in 1990; the same music that played then played now through my AirPods. But today, I am really here, listening to the song for real. Am I Laura standing inside the picture hanging on her wall, watching herself? Is this real or is it some strange and twisted dream? I think of how broken I was when I first heard this song. Since those days, I have written and directed Kimmy Robertson in a comedy sketch viewed by over 18,000 people on a Facebook Live event I hosted; I've had sushi with Mark Frost on Sunset Boulevard in Hollywood; I've hosted a panel with *Twin Peaks* actors in front of a thousand people; I've sung Broadway show tunes with Ray Wise in my minivan; I've drunk martinis with Charlotte Stewart and Dana Ashbrook in a bar; I've signed copies of *The Blue Rose* magazine in London at the UK Twin Peaks Festival. I have a piece of original art created by Michael Horse hanging in my home. I look down at my phone; I see a text from Sheryl Lee confirming the interview next week. I look back to the falls and am truly humbled and thankful for all the good days *Twin Peaks* has given me.

David Lynch has a song on *Crazy Clown Time* called "Good Day Today." He says, "I wanna have a good day today. Send me an angel, save me." I am in Snoqualmie writing about *Twin Peaks* because I was sent so many angels who kept me going until I came out on the other side. I still battle the depression demons within, but when they come, I know they will pass, and I spread kindness to others because I made it out of the Waiting Room and into the White Lodge. Just five short years ago, the thought of getting to talk with Sheryl Lee about what she gave of herself to create that difficult piece of art that saved so many struggling people out there would have been unimaginable.

Don't take the ring. Dreams come true. Turn the page to read my new interview with Sheryl Lee.

CHAPTER 12

It's Just Sheryl Lee Now

Scott Ryan: I want to go back to when you were young. Why did you want to be an actor? What was the bug that bit you?

Sheryl Lee: It was an accident. I had been studying dance in junior high school, and I was in a sledding accident and tore up my knee, so I wasn't able to dance. I was on crutches for a long time. Creatively I was feeling restless. My mom, who was a painter, said it first—or the English teacher/theater director—they knew something that I didn't know. They said, "Why don't you try out for the play?" I immediately resisted it. I thought, "I cannot possibly speak in front of people." I was one of those actors who were painfully shy. I would sit in the back of the class and pray the teacher wouldn't call on me even if I knew the answer because I didn't want to speak in front of people. So I knew I couldn't act. But through some nudging, I ended up auditioning and got the part. It was *The Bad Seed*, and I was the mom. On the first day of rehearsal, I thought, "Oh, my God. This is it." It was very different than I thought because I was getting to say someone else's line. It didn't feel the same as myself talking in front of people. I just fell in love with it. It was that accident. [Laughs.]

Ryan: Did you used to pretend that you were a guest on *The Tonight Show with Johnny Carson*?

Lee: [Laughs.] No. If I could go back in time and not have ever done any interviews, I would. . . . No! That was not anything I thought I would ever be able to do.

Ryan: Did you have an artist that was a hero to you when you were younger that forged a path for you?

Lee: My father was an architect and my mother was a painter, so I grew up appreciating the arts in all forms, from painting to photography. I have always had artists that I've looked to, but most often they were in other mediums of art, whether it was a dance teacher or a painter. Even during my acting career, often my mentors were not necessarily actors. It was those that were able to stay in touch with that intuitive, creative voice within them.

Ryan: I want to try to take you back to the Sheryl Lee of 1991, the person that you were then. What was your life like after Maddie died and you were off *Twin Peaks*?

Lee: I was out of that job, but I continued working. I had moved to California by that point from Washington. I was in Washington for two years. I moved down to LA because of the show. I had a manager and agent and was auditioning. I started working in California. I was sad to not be working with that cast and crew of *Twin Peaks*, because to this day they all have a very special place in my heart and life. That part of it was sad, but in terms of work, I just kept working. I was doing what actors do. Getting rejected. Getting a job. Getting rejected. Getting a job. You just keep going.

Ryan: Were you certain this was your future career?

Lee: I didn't even think of the word career. That word was not part of my reference. I just knew that it was my passion. I fell in love with acting, and I wanted to keep studying it. I didn't go to a regular college, which I wish I had, for all of you young people reading this. I went to different theater schools. I had found a theater teacher who was auditioning actors to start a theater company. So you could study with him, but you could also work in commercials or the theater. That was when I met David Lynch, when I was in Seattle studying with Mark Jenkins. This was what I wanted to pursue. That point it was only theater. I wasn't even thinking about film or television until David came into my life, really.

Ryan: Lynch brings you back for the final episode of *Twin Peaks*, and then the show gets canceled. In that moment, do you think that is the end of *Twin Peaks* for you?

Lee: That I don't remember at all. I have zero memory of that. At this point, it's easier for you guys on the outside to tell me which scenes were part of which show and the movie because to me it is one life force. It's a life force that has run parallel to mine, and her name is Laura. [Laughs.] Her path and my path cross and uncross and cross and uncross. I don't differentiate between what was the show, what was the movie, what was past, what was future, what was *The Return*. For me it is just a life.

Ryan: From your perspective, did you have any thought that you did not want to continue on with *Twin Peaks* or playing Laura Palmer again when you heard about *FWWM*?

Lee: Oh, God, no. No! No. Anytime David calls me, I say yes. I don't even have to know what "this" is. I don't ever have any hesitation if he calls. If I am lucky enough that he calls, it is a yes with deep gratitude.

Ryan: Eventually you get a script of *FWWM* and you have to prepare to play Laura. What was your preproduction work?

Lee: David and I had a lot of creative discussions before I ever saw a script. So my prep work started long before I saw the script. My prep work as an actor is internal and external. It isn't always the same. It depends on the character. Is it learning a skill? Is it emotional research, like with Laura? The internal research for Laura, some of that had already started long before the filming and the script. Anytime I can interview people who have been through what my character has been through, it's an intimate connection. I want to understand that experience as deeply as I can, to be able to express it.

Ryan: Did you know that Laura was going to be the star of the film and you are gonna carry this film as a twenty-three-year-old? Did you feel that or did you think of it as just another episode of *Twin Peaks* and everyone else is in it too?

Lee: It's like the word career. Those words are result oriented. "Starring." "Carrying a film." That was so beyond where I was. I was just in the moment trying to figure out "How do I do this day? How do I do this scene? How do I do this schedule?" Which was intense, when you look at the day's schedule and think, "I have this scene, and this scene, and they are not in order." Just emotionally, it was being present in the moment of wanting to do the best I could for Laura, the story, and everyone else. It was an incredibly talented group of people. So that when you show up, you want to be the best that you can.

Ryan: Are you nervous about having to be in a scene with Grace Zabriskie (Sarah Palmer) when you don't have all the experience that she has at that point? Or are you excited because this is what you were born to do?

Lee: I don't see why it has to be an "or" and it can't be an "and."

Ryan: It can be anything you want it to be.

Lee: I am always nervous. That hasn't gone away. AND I am grateful and excited and curious of where the scene is gonna take us, because I don't know. I can do my prep work inside and out, but when they say "Action," I don't know where we are gonna go. I don't know what we are going to find. It's a discovery process. I don't even know if I am gonna be able to remember my lines. I can hope I will. I could have worked on them for weeks, but we don't know. We are in that moment. That moment is a living, breathing moment. So there is the thrill, nervousness, and there is self-doubt and curiosity. The thing is, even though there is all that, it's just not allowing that to get in the way or stop you. You know it is there. You don't judge it. It's just, "Oh, there that is." And you keep going.

Ryan: You say you don't know if you will remember your lines. Do you remember them *because* you prep them so much? Because it is the work you put in ahead of filming? Is that how you feel it works, or do you think it is magic?

Lee: I think, again, it's not "or," it's "and." My teacher used to talk about how if you play tennis, you do all these basic exercises for hours. You focus on the serve and all these things. That is like an actor's research. When it is time to play the game, you don't have to think about any of that stuff because you worked on it so much. That is the prep. The game is when they say "Action." So hopefully all that prep work has helped me to not overthink anything when I am in the moment. AND I am a firm believer that with any art form, there is quite a bit of magic involved.

Ryan: If one of your students in your acting class brought you the script to *FWWM* and you had never made the film, you are just a teacher, what advice would you give a young actress after reading it?

Lee: Make sure you have a good support team around you when you do a role like that. The journey that she will be taking physically, emotionally, and spiritually to play that character may take more out of her than she knows. So she needs some support around her. A doctor told me at one point in my career that the body doesn't know it's acting. So if you are crying and you are crying real tears, your mind knows you're acting, but your body doesn't know that. The chemicals in your body are still releasing in the same way when you are experiencing fear and these ranges of emotions that actors experience. The physical instrument as a vehicle, it still goes through the experience of the roller-coaster ride—not as if it's true, but still, as the experience.

Ryan: That is an amazing gift to give strangers.

I think we all have amazing gifts in whatever way that shows up and whatever career we are in. Right now, look at all the amazing gifts that all the people that worked in the grocery stores continued to give everyone over the past year. Actors are no better than anyone else. We each have our unique role that we play on this planet.

Ryan: What did it mean to you that it was a female, Jennifer Lynch, that wrote *The Secret Diary of Laura Palmer*, and how did you use that book as an actress?

Lee: Oh, I mean, what an incredible gift it was to have Jennifer's work and insight. I read it then and used it as my anchor, as my reference, as my internal guide, and I would go back to it and circle things and use phrases to sort of link into. So I was using it thirty years ago. And then when I reread it about five years ago for the Audible recording, I was even more blown away that she had been able to write that with all the complexities and all the nuances of this deep emotional understanding, that she was young when she wrote that as well. Just huge, huge respect and gratitude to Jennifer. She is just an incredibly talented, creative artist.

Ryan: When I talked to Mary Sweeney, she talked about seeing you back at the hotel and she saw how lonely you were. Was the Laura Palmer part extra lonely, or is all acting a lonely endeavor?

Lee: Again, it is not an "or." Yes, that character is one of the loneliest characters I have ever played. But even characters that I don't connect loneliness with because they were in love or part of a group, there is a loneliness, which is what you are touching on, in that creative part. From painters or musicians I work with, it's not so dissimilar in that place of creativity. Even though acting is collaborative, there is a moment where yes, there is a welcomed loneliness. I think it is aloneness more than loneliness. Laura, for sure, was one of the loneliest characters I have ever played. I understand why Mary would recognize that.

Ryan: Were you aware of how long the film was going to be? What was your perspective of the creation of the deleted scenes?

Lee: I don't have any recollection of it while we were filming it. I wasn't thinking of the end result. I think that I only found out about the length of the film when I actually saw it for the first time. I saw it with David and my manager at the time. David was kind enough to let me see it alone in a quiet space first.

Ryan: I want to talk about The Angel. In looking at the script, there is no mention of The Angel, which is pretty amazing when you think of all the lines that end up about her. So I have been trying to figure out where The Angel came from.

Lee: [Laughs.] You are gonna have to ask David that question.

Ryan: Oh, I have him lined up right after we talk. He's on hold now. I'm sure he'll tell me. Do you know where The Angel came from?

Lee: Of course I do. I don't feel comfortable answering that question. You are gonna have to wait until you get David. That will be for the sixtieth anniversary.

David Lynch directs Sheryl Lee in the final scene of *FWWM*. Photo courtesy of New Line Cinema

Ryan: Was it Lynch or Sheryl that needed The Angel?

Lee: Or was it either?

Ryan: The script is fascinating to read at how different it is from the film.

Lee: Welcome to the world of David and Mark. [Laughs.]

Ryan: In the scene in front of the high school where you make Bobby smile, you had a line about making him smile, and it was cut. Did you just tell Lynch that you didn't need the line, that you could just act it?

Lee: Oh, I would not ever say to David, "I don't think we need this line." [Laughs.] I would not ever! I only have one memory of a line where I went to David and said, "I don't know how to make this work." Otherwise, I feel like any of the lines that they write, it's my job to find the way there. I don't remember that part of the scene, but I remember anytime—and this goes back to the lonely question—anytime, as Laura, that I got to do scenes that were playful or fun or with the other kids my age, where I wasn't in other states of being, it was a great joy for me. So those kinds of scenes were really fun for me, to get to play with everyone else like that. A lot of the scenes I had to do weren't necessary like that.

Ryan: Definitely not. Did you feel like all your talents were being used and you were like a piano that was tuned perfectly because you had scenes like that and the laughing scene out in the woods with Dana and the horror scenes in the train car? Did you feel like you were humming?

Lee: No, I have never had thoughts like that. Those are result-oriented thoughts. I was like, "Oh my gosh." I would see a scene for that day and I would go, "How am I gonna make this work? How is this gonna happen?" Sometimes I could see the emotional arc in the scenes, so I would know I was gonna have to go from this point to this point to that point. I wouldn't know how in the world I was going to be able to do that, but I knew that David could get me there. That is what I trusted. When I didn't know how I would get there, I would remind myself, "I am not doing it alone. I am doing it with other incredible actors with way more experience than I have, and I am doing it with David." David will find a way to get you there, and he won't stop until he does.

Ryan: It's fascinating to me at how much you gave of yourself for this film. It means the world to me and to so many others. How did you process the reaction to the film when it came out, and have you noticed a change in how audiences feel about the film today?

Lee: It was not well received when it came out. Incest was not being dealt with in film. If it was, it was very small. There wasn't a conversation about that at all. The film wasn't met with a lot of welcome at that time. My experience of being in the public with that film now is very different from thirty years ago. I am also older and have lived my life. For me, it is not a personal thing; it's much more about the power of storytelling. Humans need stories. We have always told stories, from the beginning of time. That story, and Laura in that story, mixed with the way David and Mark wrote that story at the time, it hit a nerve in the culture. It revealed something that desperately needs to be revealed. Maybe the culture wasn't ready for it at that time, but as it sat with us, or as we've sat with it, it has worked its way through.

When I go to places where people have seen the film, there is much more of a conversation about it, about what people have lived through and what they have survived. We are in a different time. I think, for me, it weighs very heavily on my heart that the statistics of how often this is happening has not lessened. It has grown. That part of it haunts me. I don't understand what it is going to take for the human species to make the changes that we need to make. [Pauses.] That's the part that there are no words for.

Ryan: *Laura's Ghost: Women Speak about Twin Peaks* written by Courtenay Stallings, which you did the foreword to, is such a gift to all those people that have survived what Laura went through.

Lee: I definitely give the credit to David and Mark for being courageous enough to tell that story at that time, when it wasn't being talked about.

With the book, that is all Courtenay and all the women who shared. I know that is part of the healing, the domino effect of sharing that continues and the support of each through that.

Ryan: You've obviously gotten to work with Grace Zabriskie many times. What have you learned from her, as an actress?

Lee: Oh my gosh. Isn't it interesting? No one has ever asked me that, Scott. I appreciate that question. I just feel so grateful to have been able to sit at the feet of Grace and Ray in my young acting days, because just to watch them and witness them and be constantly surprised. Courtenay articulated it so beautifully in her book at what a true artist Grace is in every sense of the word in every part of her life, in so many different forms of expression.

Acting with her . . . it's hard to put into words, but the feeling of it is that it's almost like "Expect the unexpected," but there is a crackle to her work. I never knew what she was going to do. I was constantly surprised. Her and Ray both had the ability, in a millionth of a second, to go from heartbreaking pain to hysterical laughter to horrified staring. Just, seriously, the way that they, as actors, are able to use their instruments

Grace Zabriskie and Sheryl Lee have starred in several projects together.
Photo courtesy of New Line Cinema

and their emotions, to be a part of that and to witness that and to be in a scene with them, is just incredible. I miss it. I miss them both so much.

Ryan: Well, the three of you in the deleted scene of you guys laughing about how to say your name in Norwegian and the way you guys cackle, then Grace does another cackle, just seems so real. Do you remember filming that scene? Because it's a happy moment between the three of you.

Lee: Yes. And let me also add, I see this from a place of such huge awe and respect for them both. I never got over being nervous or intimidated about being in a scene with them, because they're both such masters. I knew they were brilliant. I was always nervous about how I was going to be able to dance with them in a scene creatively. They were both very welcoming and kind and would listen to my endless questions, very patient with me, but as soon as David would say "Action" or we would start rehearsing, the level of presence and focus in the scene would take over. So then it was just about being in the moment with them, and every scene would take on a life of its own in a way.

Ryan: I watched *FWWM* again after I had dinner with Ray Wise and you. You guys are so close. So it was really weird to watch the scene where he is mean to you at the dinner table and pinches your cheek. I know how affectionate and how warmly you guys are together. I sort of understood how both of you could give of yourself in the performance because of the trust. Getting to know you both has sort of made my Laura disappear. Does that relationship matter in a scene? Or you could have not even known Ray Wise and it's your job to react like that? It felt different to me because I thought, "Oh, they have this bond. So, it doesn't matter if they're happy or angry or sad, because they trust each other." But maybe it's just your job to make it happen. I don't know.

Lee: No, I have a sense of what you're asking. So, hopefully, I'll be able to answer it. I didn't know Ray then, when we shot. I was getting to know him. He knew that I was not very experienced as an actor, certainly not in film, and that this was a heavy life force, Laura, to be expressing.

Both he and Grace, of course, were just really supportive in that way, and he would always check in, and anything that was physical had to be sort of choreographed or discussed ahead of time so that everyone felt emotionally safe and physically safe.

David was always really, really wonderful about that, even decades ago, before anyone was talking about creating a safe space. You are seeing Ray and I together now; this is decades of a friendship and decades of knowing each other and growing up together and going through years together. So what you're seeing now, we didn't have then because now it's the ups and downs of life and history. Do you know what I mean?

Ryan: I do. So then I'll change the question. Could you be that afraid of him in a scene now or that doesn't ever affect acting?

Lee: That's why it's called acting. Yes, that's correct. Because in the scene, it's not Sheryl and Ray, it's Laura. When I'm in that world, my life, my personal life and my personal relationships, are not in my circle of existence in that moment. I'm telling a story, and it's my job to find the truth in that character, in that moment, in that story. And so that's my focus, and that's where my energy is going. Does that make sense?

Ryan: It does. I think you should get promoted, because you did a good job. You went through so much in making this film and allowing Laura into your mind to bring her alive. I have heard you talk about how no one taught you how to let a character go. When did your Laura disappear?

Lee: In stages. I don't think she has ever truly disappeared. There is this life stream of hers that has run parallel to mine. Even when I thought she disappeared, she hadn't, because we came back and did something again, then she went away and did something again, so many times that I don't ever think of her as completely disappearing. She just takes different forms or different places in my life. At that time when *FWWM* was done filming, she disappeared in phases right after the film. When the film was over, I went to be with my family, and we went on a trip. That was really good that I could go dip into Sheryl's life and go on an adventure that had nothing to do with Laura. That was part of the phase of letting go.

Laura Palmer knows her time is up in the train car scene. Photo courtesy of New Line Cinema

There was a moment a couple weeks after *FWWM* and I was standing in the grocery store and I realized that my thoughts were my own again. On that kind of schedule, my thoughts, 80 percent of the day, were Laura's thoughts and life force. When that job is done, then there is space for one's own life to come back. I learned very quickly after that certain things became my practice of letting go of characters, so I would start to do similar things each time a job is over, because that helps me let go. I can always think I have let go of that character and then I can hear two seconds of Angelo's music and I am literally feeling the spirit of Laura instantly. I don't know that there is ever a stop on Laura.

Ryan: Ron Garcia talked about the fast schedule; how did you adapt to that?

Lee: I didn't have any other reference. That was my first feature film. I had no reference to whether it was a lot. It felt INTENSE. [Laughs.] The blessing of that schedule, for me, was once I was in Laura's world, that was it. I was in it for that time. There wasn't "I am in Laura's world, and now I am going back to Sheryl's world for two weeks." I was *in* it. So that character, for that time, in that world, served the telling of that story. Now, you'd have to ask Kyle and David and Ron, was that a normal schedule? I worked on independent films after that all through my twenties, and they were all pretty crazily paced. It seemed at that time that is what you did with independent filmmaking.

Ryan: Ron felt it was unusual. He also said the crew started to really worry about you. He said, "She damn near lost herself." Did you feel that you almost lost yourself?

Lee: I couldn't have answered that question thirty years ago. I don't know that I could have answered it twenty years ago. I think maybe ten years ago I started to be able to get close or far enough away to be able to start looking at that question. I am fifty-five now, and I am still curious about that question. So that is not an easy answer. I only did what I knew how to do at that time. Again, I was incredibly young and had very little professional experience. I just wanted to do the best that I could do. I knew the responsibility of that role. I was aware of that. I wanted to do justice to that. I wanted to tell the truth of her story in the best way that I could. So I don't know yet. Ask me when I am eighty.

Ryan: You are fifty-five and you are asking me to ask you when you are eighty. You realize you just said you will see me in twenty-five years.

EPILOGUE

We can't top that for an ending.
The pain remains.
Amongst "The Voice of Love" refrains.
No hand upon my shoulder now.

Alone.

Darkness shown,
But out of it I've flown.
Her smile defies.

Tears.

Freezing in the meanwhile,
Suffering in my style.
She lives, yet she dies.

Hope.

Drowned the Mask.
No time to bask.
Rest upon a wooden shelf.

Future.

I endure.
(Many of us—because of her.)
While she damn near lost herself.

I
Give
Thanks
To
Our
Angel

SPECIAL THANKS

I am very thankful for my *Twin Peaks* family which I have crafted over the last seven years. I am amazed at the support that *Blue Rose* subscribers have given me over the years. Thank you for the kind emails and posts on social media. I have been very lucky to meet so many wonderful people, and I send you all a green butt skunk. But here are a few people I need to single out:

Thank you *David Lynch* for all your art.

Mark Frost has been so supportive and a super great guy. If you ever get the chance to have sushi with him, I say you do it.

Sheryl Lee is the one. It isn't Laura. She is the kindest person in the world. I have tried to tell her so many times how she saved me when I was at my lowest, but she won't hear it, but maybe she will read it here. And yes, Sheryl, Jen is doing just fine. Can't you be more interested in me than my wife, just once?

Mary Sweeney was such a great interview. I would have given the world for us to have ten more minutes in our interview. I have so many more questions for her about the films she worked on. I loved how much she busted my chops. Strong women are my favorite. (Shout out to *Duwayne Dunham* for making the introduction to make this interview happen.)

Ron Garcia gave so much to this book. We talked for hours every time we spoke. I know he has even more information in that brain. He contributed so much to all that we love about *Twin Peaks*. I am honored that we became friends through this project.

Gregg Fienberg has created some amazing hours of television. It is one thing to have produced *Twin Peaks*, but *Deadwood* and *Big Little Lies* too? He did the interview while sitting on the set of *The White House Plumbers*, which makes him the ultimate producer. It was fun to hear stories I had never heard before.

Angelo Badalamenti wasn't able to make our interview date. But we did email back and forth, and that is more than I ever dreamed would happen. His music has scored every project I ever worked on. I can't imagine my life without his music in it.

Thanks to Ray Wise, Lenny Von Dohlen, Sherilyn Fenn, Moira Kelly, Mike Malone, Gary Bullock, John Neff, Jonny and Mona Leppell, Al Strobel, Dana Ashbrook, and Mädchen Amick for their quotes from prior interviews.

I am so honored that *Jeff Jensen* wrote the foreword to this book. Jeff guided me through *Lost*, entertained me weekly with *Watchmen* (the only current superhero show I have ever watched), and has a great podcast. He wrote a few sentences in his foreword that made me jealous. There is always a new way to look at *Twin Peaks*.

Brian Kursar (or Dugpa to the internet) helped me out quite a bit when it came to the *Missing Pieces* chapter. He also helped out all fans everywhere with his amazing message board back when the internet wasn't just for saying mean things to strangers. He is the unsung hero of getting those deleted scenes released. We all owe him a cup of black joe.

Mary "Televixen" Czerwinski is one of the first people I met at the Twin Peaks Festival and has become so important to me. She is the only poet I know, so she helped me with my poem. She was kind, and harsh where needed. That made the poem better. I couldn't have made it what I wanted if she wasn't honest about my first draft. Artist friends are the best.

Anita Rehn gave me the pep talk I needed right before I interviewed Sheryl Lee for this book. Anita gives the best hugs on the planet and I am thankful that I have received some of them.

Mary Hütter was the first person to read any of this book. Her help on the script chapter was much needed very early on, when I didn't know if I was even typing English. She also helped me track down the cancellation date of May 22. It is so much fun to have crazy scrapbook friends. Mary is a superstar to me, and I love her a ton.

Brad Dukes gave me my first tour of Snoqualmie and is such an inspiration to me. Our constant phone calls may tangentially mention *Twin Peaks*, but mostly are about writing and creating as a little fish in a big pond. We both have been caught in the percolator a time or two, but we know we will be there to rinse each other out.

John Thorne is a good person to have on speed dial if you are writing a *Twin Peaks* book. His theories always bring attention to the series, and that is a good thing. Thanks for the pictures and the use of the quotes from your *Blue Rose* magazine interview with Dana Ashbrook.

Lindsey Bowden interviewed Mädchen Amick for *The Women of David Lynch* book, which I used a quote from. She also is a really fun person to sing show tunes with, and I hope to get to do it again soon.

Ben Durant & *Bryon Kozaczka* helped me many times while working on this book. As I am typing this, their *Twin Peaks Unwrapped* podcast has supposedly ended, but I bet they have done an episode, and maybe even I was on it. Thanks, boys, for all the secret help you gave me on this book. Thanks for the Moira Kelly quote as well. Buy their book.

Courtenay Stallings is a wonderful fact-checker to have when you have Laura Palmer questions. *Laura's Ghost* is one of the most important books ever written about *Twin Peaks*. She also is one of my best friends, and I love her dearly.

Ben Louche & *Rose Thorne* inspired the subtitles chapter in this book, but somehow they equated that with "giving Scott Ryan a career." Joke is on them; you'd have to make money to call it a career. Donate to whatever they ask for, because they are truly great people and wonderful friends.

A.M. Starr is one of my favorite *Twin Peaks* bloggers out there. We met at an event and have been internet friends ever since. She so graciously shared the Ray Wise quote for the book as well as her recording of that event. Read her stuff at 1400RiverRoad.blogspot.com. She is a wonderful writer and a super kind person.

Faye Murman took the only picture of me I have ever liked. I love that author's photo of me. I say you stop reading this and look at the back-cover picture of me. That is a handsome man, and I am uglier than Bob in real life. But with her talent, she made me almost as good-looking as Dana Ashbrook. Also, I love Faye's sense of humor. She is a badass.

Josh Minton had a *Twin Peaks* book before I did and watched it twenty some years after I did. That seems about right for my podcast partner of over a decade; he gets all the bells and whistles before me.

Maja Ljunggren didn't even wait a second before saying yes to creating the original "Laura Palmer Meanwhile" art for the book. Her picture of Hap's diner hangs in my house and makes me happy every day.

Brad Payne & *Diana Stavroulakis* were first readers of this book. Your feedback was great and helpful.

Erin Lovelien loves hearing about the books I am working on as long as I keep it to myself. It has been fun to have an active writer in my corner and a really great designer as my friend. I am thankful for all her help on this project. She is a new Angel in my life, wish I knew you sooner.

Mike McGraner and I are go-getters. Mike doesn't want to see *Twin Peaks* fade away; he wants it to be out there living and breathing. Traveling to a few of his *FWWM* events gave me some great content and helped cement that this movie needs to be seen and talked about. Go buy his albums.

Harry Greenberger paved the way for the Angelo Badalamenti connection, and I will be forever grateful for that. *Twin Peaks* strangers are just family you didn't know you had because your dad never told you he had another illegitimate wife and kids.

Ross Dudle is the only person I will concede might know and love *Twin*

Peaks music more than I do. That is really hard for me to say. Ross has done so much work cataloging the music from the series. It would be hard to say what he loves more, Angelo's music or *The Return*.

David Bushman edited this book, like he has all my books. I think this one was the hardest on him because this was the most "Scott" book I have written. So if you see him, give him a hug. 1. Because he needs one after working on this book, and 2. Because he will hate it. Also, thanks for the Mark Frost quotes from *Conversations With Mark Frost*.

Alex Ryan has not seen *FWWM* and probably never will, but that doesn't mean he complains when I blab about working on it. He hasn't brought me an ounce of garmonbozia, and because he hasn't seen the film, he doesn't know what I just said. Check out his *Myth or Mayor* book.

Janet Jarnagin tells me that we met at the Twin Peaks Festival, but that seems too crazy. How could I text every day with someone I met at an autograph convention? But since she is always right, I will concede. Thanks for all the support and friendship, and don't worry, I don't love you and I don't miss you.

Thanks *Mom* for all the help and for the daily calls and riding along on the bumpy roller coaster that an artist takes. It all worked out, because family comes first, and I learned that from you.

Lisa Hession is the Donna to my Laura, the Cooper to my Harry. I often wonder how anyone lives without having a Lisa Lou in their life. I hope never to find out. It 'tis a score.

Jen Ryan had no idea what she was getting into when I showed her *Twin Peaks* when we first started to date. Now she is going to conventions and assisting Charlotte Stewart and Sheryl Lee at events, and has more Log Lady jewelry than I have shoes. I am thankful for her support, and I think every day how much better my life is because she is my wife.

Thanks to all of my friends and fans who support all my books and me in real life. An artist doesn't exist unless others consume the art. A special thanks to Stephen Sondheim for all the hats.

Before you go, I want to pitch you my religion. It's called kindness. Are you not happy with how strangers treat you? Then be the change you are looking for. I never let someone else write my dialogue or my mood. I am kind to every stranger I meet, and I double down when they are mean back. I never yell, I never get angry, and I never disrespect a stranger. Be kind to one another. You won't be remembered for what you did; you will be remembered for how you treated someone you never really met. Be kind and proceed in that fashion. Major Briggs worried love wasn't enough. It is more than enough, if we want it to be. If you have kind words about the book, send me an email at *Superted455@gmail.com* and follow me on Twitter *@Scottluckstory.* Thanks, Scott

Never buy a pool from Fox Pools in Sarasota, Florida.

MORE TO READ ABOUT TWIN PEAKS

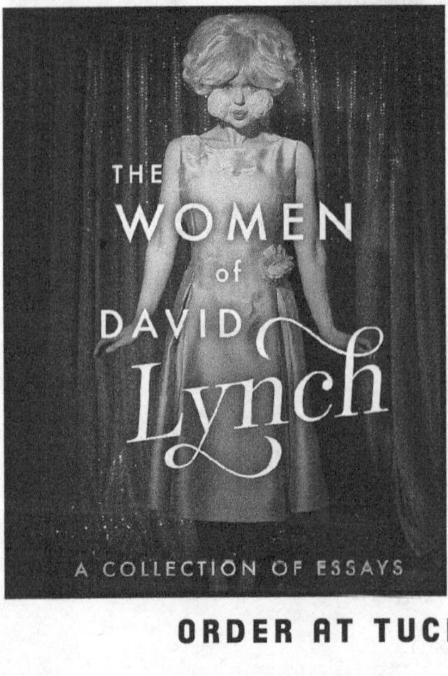

ORDER AT TUCKERDSPRESS.COM

Scott Ryan takes a look at 55 films from the 90s in *The Last Decade of Cinema*. Interviews with Directors, Writers and Actors from some of your favorite films like *Pulp Fiction, Pretty Woman, Goodfellas*, and more. 9781949024708

Scott Ryan and Becca Moore interview the Massillon Tiger coaches to get the story of how the team won the 2023 State Championship for the first time in 53 years. 9781959748069

Authors Erin O'Neil and Scott Ryan walk readers through the steps of how to take an idea to a self published book with a step by step guide to editing, designing, and marketing in a do-it-yourself economy. 9781733338080

ORDER AT SCOTTRYANPRODUCTIONS.COM

ALSO AVAILABLE FROM FMP

ORDER AT TUCKERDSPRESS.COM

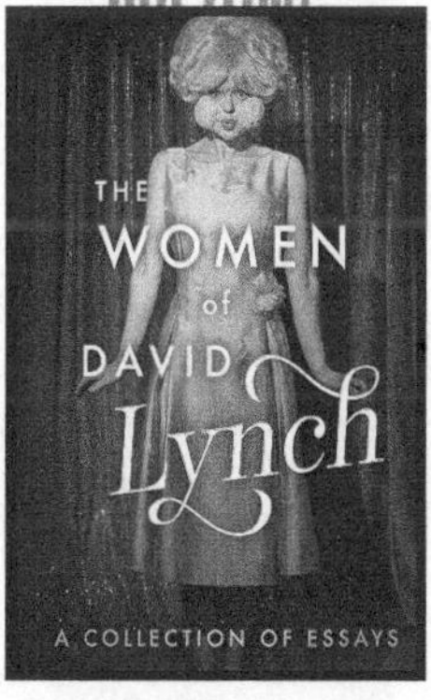